TEEN GIRLS' COMEDIC MONOLOGUES THAT ARE ACTUALLY FUNNY

TEEN GIRLS' COMEDIC MONOLOGUES THAT ARE ACTUALLY FUNNY

Edited by

ALISHA GADDIS

APPLAUSE
THEATRE & CINEMA BOOKS
An Imprint of Hal Leonard Corporation

Published in 2015 by Applause Theatre & Cinema Books
An Imprint of Hal Leonard Corporation
7777 West Bluemound Road
Milwaukee, WI 53213

Trade Book Division Editorial Offices
33 Plymouth St., Montclair, NJ 07042

Printed in the United States of America

Book design by UB Communications

Library of Congress Cataloging-in-Publication Data

Names: Gaddis, Alisha, editor.
Title: Teen girls' comedic monologues that are actually funny / edited by
    Alisha Gaddis.
Description: Milwaukee, WI : Applause Theatre & Cinema Books, an
    imprint of Hal Leonard Corporation, 2015.
Identifiers: LCCN 2015038654 | ISBN 9781480396807 (pbk.)
Subjects: LCSH: Monologues—Juvenile literature. |
    Acting—Auditions—Juvenile literature. | Comedy sketches—Juvenile
    literature.
Classification: LCC PN2080 .T4855 2015 | DDC 812/.0450817—dc23
LC record available at http://lccn.loc.gov/2015038654

www.applausebooks.com

Contents

Introduction

Ladies, you are holding this book in your hands because I was you once.

I wanted more. I wanted my big chance! I wanted to shine!

And I was a teenager.

I get it.

Whether you are in a small school's thespian group, are vying for a spot in the regional musical, or are my neighbor down the road in Hollywood—this book will help you book the part, make them laugh, and steal the show!

This book is a tool that will help you be the best comedic actress you can be by performing the funniest pieces out there. It's written by seriously funny people—successful actors, big-deal writers, and creative powerhouses.

We want you to win. Win it all—the whole enchilada!

I believe in your dreams. I believe in you!

Now go out there and make 'em laugh!

Alisha Gaddis

Seven Minutes to Heaven

Alisha Gaddis

ZANNY, 13 to 15

ZANNY is inside the basement office of her friend Emma's dad, as a result of the bottle landing on her during the 7 Minutes in Heaven game. She is with her biggest crush, Brenden.

ZANNY   Wow. I have never really been in Emma's dad's office before. There is a lot of wood paneling, huh? Is that a stuffed pheasant? Gross. What is his job anyway? . . . I don't even know.

[*Awkward beat.*]

So . . . you come here much? Just kidding. I know you don't—I mean, unless you do. Which is totally cool, too.

[*Awkward beat.*]

This game is kinda ridiculous. You know? I mean—7 Minutes in Heaven? That is so retro. Who even does this anymore? I mean—I have Tinder on my phone. One swipe and it is like seven minutes in heaven every seven seconds. Right? I mean—lame-o.

But this is Emma's party and she totally thought it would be adorbs fun. Gotta do what the party girl wants!

Is that Jägermeister? Gross. I mean—not gross that you are drinking—that's totally cool. . . . I'm not like judging you, but it totally tastes gross. It's a manly drink, but you are manly, so I guess that makes sense. It tastes like licorice—I tried it at Scott's pool party and yuck—it reminds me of the time my friends and I were on the Gravitron at the fair and the carnie who was running it got arrested for operating heavy machinery while being wasted and they cuffed him and took him away and NO ONE remembered to turn off the Gravitron and we were spinning and spinning and Hannah flipped out and was crying and some guy who was totally like twenty-five barfed on everything and his vomit flew in the air and started spinning and landed on everyone! It was disgusting and we couldn't move and the ride kept going and it smelled like Red Vines. Exactly like Jäger. Traumatizing.

[*Beat.*]

Sure, I'll have a sip . . .

[*Beat.*]

I knew you were going to be here tonight. I mean—not in a creepy stalker way, but Gavin told Gabby that you guys were getting a ride together and Gabby was so excited about Gavin that she told all us girls and asked if she could borrow my acid-washed Jeggings—so I knew that you were going to be here. But don't tell Gavin what I said about Gabby. And since you and me are in the same chemistry dissection group—it's like—wow—we are seeing each other a lot.

Chemistry right?!? GROSS. But chemistry is totally important, too . . .

[*Awkward silence.*]

So—when you were spinning that bottle and it landed on me, what did you think? I mean—don't answer that. OH god! Why did I say that? How many minutes do we have left?

[*Beat.*]

Sure, I will have another sip. I kinda like it a little bit more.

[*Drinks.*]

[*Laughing.*] Our hands totally bumped . . . sorry. I don't mind, though—if you don't. I mean—I knew you were going to be here so I hoped the bottle would land on me. But I know you are on-again, off-again with Reagan, but she was totally hooking up with Armen last week and I hope someone told you because you deserve better. And I am not saying I am better—but I would totally never hook up with Armen.

Gross—right?!?

[*Beat.*]

You want me to take a drink and then swallow it and then you want to taste it on my lips? Ha-ha-ha! Gross . . . right?

Oh—you are serious. Okay. Wow. Ummm. Our time is almost up.

But you know I am learning to love the taste of licorice I guess, and I am really glad the bottle landed on me, and I for one don't care that you are failing math.

Here—hand me the bottle . . .

[*There is a knock on the door. Reacts to knock.*]

HOLD ON!!! THIS IS ALMOST MY TIME IN HEAVEN!!! MAKE IT EIGHT MINUTES FOR CHRISTSAKES—COME BACK WHEN I SAY SO. THE BOTTLE LANDED ON ME!!!

[*Beat.*]

So, where were we—I just love playing games.

Horse Competition

Alessandra Rizzotti

JELENA, 14

JELENA is exceptionally smart and most likely has anxiety and Asperger's. Her horse calms her down. She talks to a stable boy at her horse's stable, but he is half listening.

JELENA The national thoroughbred contest is next week and Maybelle and I are not ready yet. Her ankles are broken so basically we're not going to make the high jumps. The only thing she has going for her is a really great French braid. I've been weaving sparkly hemp and flowers into her mane and I'm pretty sure she has a bigger chance if they're the type of judges that put vanity on a pedestal over athleticism. The world does that, doesn't it? I mean looks sorta win over everything these days. I'm pretty sure I know that because Tommy doesn't like me because I have brown hair, but he likes Angel because she has blonde hair. It makes sense. He hasn't ever talked to me, but hair is the only thing that's different between Angel and I, from what I can tell. I don't talk to Angel that much, but from history class, I can tell she gets As like I do, so we must be the same.

I asked my dad if he could get me a new horse for the contest, but he said Maybelle was a winner even if she didn't win the contest, so I'm going to trust him since any daddy's girl should. Do you know that thoroughbreds evolved in Britain in the seventeenth and eighteenth centuries because the English liked racing, but a thoroughbred's pedigree can be traced back to only three Arabian stallions who didn't even race, so who knows why they ever became racers. It's like, why should Maybelle even be judged on her racing abilities?

Ugh. Maybelle should probably not enter in this contest. A lot of it involves jumping and she can't do that, so what's the point? Maybe next year. I hate not having the faith in my horse, but physiological demands that could potentially hurt her health long-term are worth paying attention to. Too bad because she's energetic and her face is chiseled, which are some of the main attributes they judge thoroughbreds on, which I know because I took a horse physiology course at a barn in the Hamptons and we did a whole class on skull structure.

Last week, Maria told me her thoroughbred Macy (like Macy's the department store), had constipation, so I doubt she'll be competing. Maybe it's just not a good year for any of us really *dedicated* competitors? I won a blue medal last year, so that's okay, but what will that say about college applications in three years if I have a gap year? I'm sorta freaking out. I have nothing to show for this year. I was sorta banking on this to be my one accomplishment that I could feature in my end-of-the-year review that my father conducts on the first of January and now I have nothing. Whew. I need to breathe. Not everyone is as accomplished as I am. I have mastered twenty horse jumpings, fifty national eventing and dressage events, and I'm getting a certification in training rescued horses at the barn down the street—which not every fifteen-year-old can say, by the way. Everything is going to be okay.

What? Are you serious? Scarlett is entering into the horse jump this year???? What made her think she could do that? What kind of loyalty is that, knowing that Maybelle is not doing well this year? I thought my cousin would know that entering a contest without me would be inappropriate, but now I know who my REAL family is.

I appreciate you letting me know. What's your name again? Do you clean Scarlett's barn every day like mine? You do? If I give you twenty bucks, will you let the horseshit just stew for a few days there? I'd appreciate it. Blame it on overfeeding. I'm off! Scarlett won't win. She doesn't deserve it. Oh, I am just angryyyy right now! Ohhhhh jeez! Don't tell her I talked to you. She'll know the shit was from me. Here's the twenty. I'll give you another next time I'm back at the barn. Don't be frivolous and waste the cash on anything but your college tuition. You don't want to be a stable boy forevs.

Circus Runaway

Leah Mann

AMARYLLIS, 14 to 16

AMARYLLIS, *an acrobat and entertainer extraordinaire, yells up at her twin brother, FLAVIO, who soars overhead, above the ring inside a huge circus tent.*

AMARYLLIS   Flavio, I have to talk to you.

Flavio! I mean it, I'm not yelling up at you for this whole conversation! Get off the damn trapeze and talk to me!

[*Beat.*]

Of course it's important—isn't your twin sense tingling!? Man, we are all out of sync . . .

[FLAVIO *ignores her, soaring from one trapeze to another high above her head.*]

Ay dios.

[AMARYLLIS *shouts up to him, her eyes following as he swings back and forth above her.*]

Don't freak out, okay, promise? I didn't freak out when you started dating the bearded lady and she's loca. So now you got to be cool. Okay?

[*Beat.*]

No, I'm not hooking up with Alfonse! He's all bulging and gross. I'm sorry, but just because you a strong man don't mean you a handsome man. . . . No, what I got to say is bigger than that.

[AMARYLLIS *takes a deep breath.*]

I'm running away.

[FLAVIO*'s grip slips—he nearly falls.*]

I said don't freak!

[FLAVIO *catches himself.* AMARYLLIS *sighs deeply.*]

We're seventeen now and I want to join the real world. I'm tired of the circus. I hate it here. I want to go to college and live in a room that's not on wheels. I want friends, not this weird troupe of people who are family and friends and coworkers. There's no boundaries, no privacy, no freedom here. Just because you and Mama and Papi are part of this world, doesn't mean I have to be. There is so much more out there. . . . Stop looking at me like I'm crazy. I don't want to be an acrobat! Okay? Not everyone wants to go flyin' through the air like a freakin' rabid monkey.

[*Offended,* FLAVIO *swings himself up, somersaults onto another trapeze and heads to the opposite end of the tent.* AMARYLLIS *hurries after him, trying to catch up.*]

I'm trying to be normal, you know what I'm saying? Like I want to wear jeans every day. I've thought about it long and hard—don't be thinking this is easy—but I have to do this for me. I'm suffocating here and I know my true calling—

I want to be a dermatologist.

I'm telling you, it's sweet. You make bank, have regular hours, benefits, a 401(k)! I'll be Doctor Amaryllis, all on my own, not half of "The Amazing Amaryllis & Fabulous Flavio, the Terrifyingly Twisty Twins!"

Don't you ever just want to be "Flavio, the guy who makes killer chili"? Don't you want to be Flavio, individual, with his own unique personality? Aren't you tired of being everyone else's entertainment?

I am.

How are we supposed to even know who we are if we're never apart? Where do I end and you start?

[*Beat.*]

I know I end before any of your bits that been messin' with the bearded lady, but you know what I'm sayin'? Who's Amaryllis? Does she like Indian food? Is she good at calculus? I don't know! I know I look good in a leotard, I know I can sew sequins, muck out the stables, and ride a tiger—but that's it . . . useless!

[FLAVIO *takes off in the opposite direction and she jogs after him again.*]

I'm tired of snake charmers, elephants, and cotton candy. Just the smell of popcorn and churros makes my stomach hurt. I don't want to ride into work on an albino Arabian stallion with a diamond headdress on—I want a little four-door sedan with seat warmers and good gas mileage.

I don't want acrobatics training seven hours a day—I want to take a spin class.

[AMARYLLIS *gives up trying to stay with* FLAVIO *and sits down on the floor, talking as much to herself as to him now.*]

Bro, it sounds awesome—you wear whatever you want, like shorts or whatever, and bring a water bottle and sit on a bike in an

air-conditioned gym while a teacher tells you to go faster or slower
and there's music but no choreography or special effects.

And it's not like we even see the world. We see the same damn
tents and games and porta-potties in every town. People's clothes
change and maybe like, in one place the people have more tattoos
and in another they mostly white or they mostly black, but that's
not travel—that's just driving around.

I want to experience things! I want to wake up and buy Starbucks
on the way to class; I want to have study groups and go on dates. I
want to catch up with friends over drinks at a bar and then walk
back to my apartment and curl up with a cat—not a Bengali
tiger . . . a normal cat that doesn't do any tricks—and watch reality
TV. I want to wait in line at the DMV to get my driver's license
and have a permanent address. I want to walk out on the street
without Madame Mariana telling me to watch out for a man in a
red coat and black goatee because she saw something ominous in
her tarot cards. If I trip in a pothole or some dude in a coat gets up
in my business, no biggie. Let it be a surprise! Besides, it's always
just Ringmaster Ferdinand being a jerk. Like someone else in a red
coat and black goatee is hanging around waiting to cause
trouble . . . Madame Mariana is weak.

[FLAVIO *is now twisting and twirling directly above her.*]

Don't be mad. I know I'm ruining the act, but you can find another
twin . . .

[*Beat.* AMARYLLIS *gets up and looks straight up at her brother.*]

You can have your own act! We ain't even identical. I got to flatten
my boobs and you're always dying your hair so we look the same.
It's stupid. My boobs want to be free, not all wrapped up and
hidden.

[*Beat.*]

Flavio . . . I'm sorry. But it's decided. Don't tell Mama and Papi yet, I need a head start.

[FLAVIO *does a flip off the trapeze landing neatly in front of her. AMARYLLIS follows his dismount with her head. Her face softens when he lands in front of her.*]

I love you. I'll miss you, I'll think of you every time I look in the mirror, but I gotta roll . . . adventure is waiting.

Cincinnati, I'm coming at you!

[AMARYLLIS *cartwheels and tumbles away from her brother.*]

I, Babysitter

Bri LeRose

ERIN McCARTHY, 15

ERIN McCARTHY, *an enthusiastic, theatrical girl, sits addressing a "woman" next to her in the back seat of a car.*

ERIN   I am an excellent babysitter. I am Mary Poppins. I am Maria from *The Sound of Music*. I am Julie Andrews in real life, plus diaper skills and CPR certification. You need the kids to eat more vegetables? I'm your girl. You need to keep the little tykes occupied outside while the carpets get cleaned? I'm all over it. You need gluten-free, sugar-free, construction-themed cupcakes for Jack's third birthday party, and you need them *now*?! Where's the apron, lady? I've got work to do.

Yes, I do it all. Cooking, cleaning, crafting, reading, role-playing, wrestling, ready-to-eat healthy snack making—and I do it with a smile. For ten bucks an hour, you can buy yourself some peace of mind, knowing that your kids are in the hands of a cool, capable girl, and she has your pediatricians on speed dial, just in case.

Now, you're probably asking yourself, how does she do it? No, no, *why* does she do it? Why does she subject herself to hair pulling, spitting, and steady streams of poo for a few measly dollars a night? Isn't there a TJ Maxx or a Dairy Queen that'll take her in? Well, folks, I do it for one simple reason: I do it for the stories.

That's right, I'm using your children as ammo for my future one-woman show. I add every bizarre thing they do, every strange thought they scream out to the world, into my memory log of future characters and one-liners to draw on someday when it's my time to shine. My business is collecting weirdness. And lady? Business is good.

Did you know your daughter keeps her finger in her nose just because she can? There aren't even any boogers up there; she ate them all. But she keeps that finger up there for ten to twelve minutes at a time, holding entire conversations with that thing jammed up to the second knuckle. [ERIN's *finger is in her nose; she puts on a kid voice.*] "UM, I HAVE AN IDEA. LET'S GO LOOK AT MY PET SNAIL AND THEN WE CAN PLAY BABY. HEY, DO YOU HAVE A BOYFRIEND?" No, little lady, I don't have a boyfriend. But I do have a cash cow right in front of me, trying to reach her brain with her index finger.

Do you have any idea how much your kid loves butts? Your toddler is the Sir Mix-a-Lot of his playgroup, ma'am, and he has no idea that it's inappropriate. I need all my fingers and all my toes and probably some of your daughter's booger-covered fingers too just to count the number of times your son has tried to lift up my skirt. He says, "I wanna see your butt, B. I wanna see your butt." He pounds on the bathroom door when he knows I'm in there, dying to get a peek. Oh god, if he could just *see* my butt. If he could just *know* what it's like, even for a second, everything would be right in his simple, little world. Honestly? I think you should consider putting parental controls on the Nicki Minaj video hour on Fuse, ma'am.

And your *other* daughter? The older one who runs around shirtless, screaming, "I. AM. PANTS MAN!!!"? She's already named all of the various characters I'll be stealing. Here is a list of

names she's given herself or her siblings when we play family:
Jaymith. Goloba. Herbert. Bounda. Bubblester. Shi-shi. And of
course, played with grace by your butt-obsessed three-year-old
Jack, the one, the only . . . Dr. Baby. I plan to fully embody the
role of Dr. Baby, and let me tell you, I can smell the Tony Awards
now.

But of course, every show needs a bit of drama. Some conflict.
Some real, human struggle to carry us through the emotional
roller coaster that is the theater. Well, your oldest daughter has
certainly provided that. Allow me to set the stage: the other day I
was leaving, saying good-bye to your children, who were,
understandably, sad to see me and my sparkling energy walk
through that door at the end of the night. They're frantically
grabbing at my pants, hiding my cell phone, and hooking
themselves to my leg like a barnacle to a great white whale.
Finally, I shake them off, get my wad of cash, and head toward
the door. But then, at the eleventh hour, as her little brain is
working overtime to find something, anything, to get me to stay,
your daughter screams, "YOU POOPED!" And I stop, look at
her, and ask, "When, specifically?" She scrambles. "You pooped
all over our furniture!" We have a tender moment where I squat
down, grab her shoulders, and explain to the little cherub that,
"No, honey, I did *not* poop all over your furniture. It's time for
me to go now, but I'll be back real soon. Whenever your mother
needs to go to book club, I'll be there. Whenever your father
needs to watch college basketball with the door closed, I'll be
there. Whenever your parents need to pretend they're on a
business trip, when really they just get a room at the Holiday Inn
down the street, I'll be there. And I'll bring the board games."

So all that being said, Mrs. Adams, I'm actually raising my rate to
twelve dollars an hour. I know it's a sizable jump, but considering

the sense of nostalgia and glory that is sure to be brought to your family somewhere down the line, when they become characters and plot points in major theatrical productions, it's really quite a steal when you think about it, no?

Thanks for the ride home!

[ERIN *mimes getting out of a car and takes a bow.*]

No Place Like Home

Keisha Cosand

MANDY, 18

MANDY *is in the living room of her parents' house, talking to them about not moving out.*

MANDY   Mom, Dad, remember how I said I hate you, and I'm out of here the second I turn eighteen. About that . . . first, I would like to apologize. I don't really HATE you. You'll be pleased to know that I've been giving this A LOT of thought.

As much as I would LOVE to move out and have my own apartment, and as great as it would be to decorate it super cool with IKEA everything, and have parties . . . invite all the guys you don't approve of and won't let me go out with . . . I mean just because Donny has tattoo sleeves and his tongue is pierced doesn't make him a bad guy. [MANDY *pauses and lets out a happy sigh.*] I could sleep-in forever and have a freezer full of ice cream. No one would yell at me when I don't make my bed, and I could come and go any time of the day or night. It really would be heaven. I wouldn't have to worry about leaving dishes in the sink, or you guys waiting up for me at midnight, in the La-Z-Boy, in the dark . . . seriously, I thought I was going to have a heart attack when you swiveled around and beamed that flashlight in my face! You have to agree, you guys are a little extreme.

But like I said, I've been thinking . . . and doing some math. Don't give me that look, Dad, I can add (on my phone). Apartments are totally expensive! A decent place in a neighborhood with a moderately low crime rate is $1,200 a month! Then food will run about $200, if I never eat out, and gas is like $150. Where am I going to get that kind of money? That doesn't even include clothes, makeup, hair, and just forget about my nails! Yes, I know, I'm supposed to work, but I looked into that. The only jobs I'm qualified for pay like $8 an hour. Do you know it would take me almost twenty hours of hard labor to buy a pair of jeans?! Yes, Mom, I know your jeans don't cost that much, and no offense, but I wouldn't be caught dead in jeans from the Gap.

So . . . I think you will be excited to know that I am not moving out. I am going to stay here with you guys after all! Isn't this great? Um, I am hoping that you will be open to a few compromises, though. Now that I'm an adult, I think we should ditch the curfew. Oh, and I think you will agree that it's time to increase my allowance. Honestly, I think this is best for all of us. You guys get to keep your little girl . . . FOREVER! YAY! Group hug?

The Future Missed Connection

Gina Nicewonger

DANIELLE, 16 to 19

In the interior of a grocery store, in the chip aisle.

DANIELLE   Ah-ha. I knew it. You can talk to me. It's okay. You've been following me. I know because I saw you in the candy aisle and skipped to the chip aisle as a test. You might as well save the trouble. You're just going to wind up writing a Missed Connection later.

Yes, "like on Craigslist." More people use Craigslist for misconnections than to sell their furniture. You'll end up posting about how you followed a beauty wearing a sexy purple hoodie and we even bought the same salsa. Yeah, Old El Paso! Weird, right?

Fine, don't ask me out, but this is going to be so annoying later. Because when you read a bunch of Missed Connections, they all start to seem familiar. I start to think, was I at the Starplex 7 on Saturday? Did I open the door for a stranger and smile? And then I have to meet everyone, just in case.

Oh, the silence is killing me. Fine. I WILL grab a Jamba Juice with you!

You don't want juice? But, I don't do dinner on first dates. Oh my god, our baskets just brushed!

[Quoting a future post.]

"We checked out at the exact same time. Our shopping baskets gently kissed."

Alright! If you say so. I'll leave you alone. I just thought we had so much in common. I mean, how many people drink diet Dr Pepper?

[Shocked.]

What? It's for your girlfriend?!

[Announcing loudly.]

Attention, Ladies! For all you Craigslist users out there: Do not trust your boyfriend on his own anywhere! He will use any opportunity to pick up random hot chicks. Despite the fact that he has a GIRLFRIEND!

[To man.]

Who do you think you are, anyway?

[DANIELLE *begins to leave, but then returns.*]

Seriously though, if you break up with your girlfriend, remember—purple hoodie. I'll be checking.

[DANIELLE *exits.*]

Band Practice

Carla Cackowski

MARISA, 15

MARISA *talks to her two best friends in the lunchroom at school about starting a band.*

MARISA   You guys, our band is not just gonna be any normal kind of band. We're not gonna be one of those bands that just like, plays gigs, makes albums, and sells merch at the merch table. We're gonna be one of those bands that starts a whole new genre of music!

Angela, do you play drums? No? It's okay. Do you play bass? Not a problem. How about keyboard? Really? Not that, either? No worries, no worries. What about you, Nicole? What instruments do you play? Nada. Hmm.

Me? Oh. Well, I don't play anything, either . . . yet! But I will. I will totally learn. How hard can it be? It's not like Chrissie Hynde came out of her mother's womb playing guitar. It's not like that . . . is it? No, I didn't think so. At a certain point Chrissie Hynde made a choice to play guitar and then she learned how to do it. So, that's like me right now. I'm making a choice to play guitar and then I'll learn how to do it and then our band will start a revolution!

Angela, you should play drums. Well, you have stronger arms than Nicole. Oh come on, I didn't say you have manly arms—I

said your arms are strong. Like you could kick my ass if you
wanted. But please don't. Angela, there are so many rad women
who've played drums in awesome bands. Yes there are! Moe
Tucker. Kate Schellenbach. Um, hello, Meg White! Angela, you
could totally be the next Meg White! She's not crazy. She just
doesn't leave her house or talk to other people anymore. Come
on, please? Fine. Nicole, you'll play drums. No? Why not? Ugh!
Okay! I'll play drums! And guitar. I'll play both drums and guitar
and I'll kick ass at both of 'em!

Which instruments do you want to play? Harp . . . well, that's not
very punk. Angela, do you even own a harp? Where are you
going to get a harp from? No, I don't have drums or a guitar yet.
I see your point. Okay, no problem. Angela, you'll play harp. And
what about you, Nicole? Banjo? [*Rolls eyes.*] Fine, you guys win.
You will play harp, and you will play banjo. I'll play guitar and
drums . . . This is really shaping up into something spectacular. I
mean . . . subversive! Our band is gonna kill it!

I wrote down some band names to run past you two . . .

How about "Punches in the Face"? Too vague? Okay. What do
you think of "We Will, We Will Punch You"? Or "Knuckle
Sandwiches"? How about "Hammer, Pummel, Pound, Punish"?
No? Okay, last one: "Stab-Stab-Cut-Cut" . . . "Stab-Stab-Cut-
Cut" it is!

And now for some really exciting news. I've booked our first
show! It's in two weeks, at my aunt and uncle's twentieth-
anniversary party. We've all gotta start somewhere, you know? I
once read that Hole's first gig was at Courtney Love's neighbor's
bat mitzvah. If we say yes to opportunity, success will be our
bitch. I'm pretty sure that's a direct quote from a Bikini Kill song.
Anyway, playing at this anniversary party will be a great

opportunity for us. My uncle's best friend will be there, and he once auditioned to be a second guitarist for Soundgarden in the nineties. He could totally mentor us and introduce us to the "right" people.

Of course we're ready. Do you think Sleater-Kinney sat around talking about playing music, or do you think they just went out and played that shit? Angela, Nicole, it's going to be fine. Two weeks from now is a lifetime away. Think about what we were doing two weeks ago. Angela, you were dating that loser Aidan and Nicole and I were wearing vintage aprons like they were skirts. That feels like a million-jillion years ago! In just two short weeks from now, we could be masters of our craft. We'll just have to skip school to practice. Relax, Angela. We won't need to skip every day to become masters. Just like twice. You guys, I'm seriously not worried about this gig. I already have our outfits picked out. Black dresses, fishnets, fake blood, lots of spikes. We're gonna slay them!

[MARISA *makes the rock 'n' roll hand sign and sticks out her tongue like Gene Simmons.*]

Rock 'n' roll!

Okay, let's get out of here. I have to go home and download some of the songs we're going to copy. I mean, cover. The industry term for what we're about to do is *cover*. Yeah, we're so industry now. Just like Joan Jett!

Help Me, Obi-Wan Kenobi

Margaret Finnegan

TEENAGE PRINCESS LEIA, 13 to 15

Teenage PRINCESS LEIA *is sending a holographic message to Obi-Wan Kenobi. Her hair is done up in her famous "cinnamon roll" side buns.*

PRINCESS LEIA   General Kenobi: Years ago you served my father in the clone wars; now I beg you to help me in my gravest hour of need. My dad wants to send me to Combat Survival for Princesses Camp. It's totally unfair. And it's all the fault of this kid, Duke Akbar.

What happened was this: Yesterday, the Akbars came over for dinner, and my dad and Admiral Akbar were all, "In the days of the republic, blah, blah, blah, boring, boring, boring . . ." I look next to me and the Akbars' kid—this boy, Duke, who's my age and has these giganto fish lips and eyeballs the size of probe droids—has his face in his plate. He's sucking back about a pound of linguini and clams. The noodles are all running down his chin. Total grodo.

I'm all, "Use the fork, Duke!"

The table goes silent and everybody stares at me—like I'm the disgusting one.

Then my dad says, "Not everyone can use the fork, you know." And he kind of points with his eyes to Duke's arm. Only then do I notice that all the Akbars have these little fin things instead of hands.

I mean—duh—someone could have warned me; I can't notice everything. I mean, sometimes I wish I were adopted. My parents think they're all perfect and I'm this total rebel. Besides, fork or no fork, Duke Akbar is a total nerf herder. I mean use a straw or something. No one wants to see your face in linguini.

But, Mr. Kenobi, it gets worse. Duke Akbar turns to me, and he says, "Hey, your royal worshipfulness, how about a cinnamon bun?"

And I'm all, "Oh! Cinnamon buns. Where?"

He grabs my hair and yells, "On your head!"

Obviously, I have no choice but to throw him out of his chair and gouge my nails into his fish lips. Midgouge, this little green dude appears from nowhere. He pulls me off Duke, saying "Stop! Anger leads to hate. Hate leads to violence. Violence leads to suffering."

"Yeah," I say. "That's sort of the point."

And Duke says, "You know what's pointed? Your cinnamon bun head." So what else can I do but take the fork I'm holding and whale it at him? Then, the little green dude jumps on the table and stares at my dad: "Hmmm. With her the fork is strong."

My dad just nods up and down, up and down, and the next thing you know, he says, "You're going to Combat Survival for Princesses Camp." Combat survival: Like I'll ever need that! I live on Alderan. It's a peaceful planet!

Look, you've got to talk to my dad, Obi-Wan Kenobi. He is always saying how you are really wise and stuff. He has your action figure on his bedside table. If anyone can convince him to let me stay on Alderan and live a normal princess life, it's you. Trust me: Obi-Wan Kenobi, you are my only hope.

The Grim Gardener

Bri LeRose

LIZ LOCKRIDGE, 17

LIZ LOCKRIDGE *is at a poetry slam at a coffee shop.*

LIZ   Thank you for coming here today. Poetry is a window to the souls of humankind, and tonight, I invite you to take a peek through my window. Usually, the glass is cloudy, or cracked by the storm that is life. But tonight, friends and supporters, I have grabbed the metaphorical bottle of Windex, and I assure you a clear view. This poem is one that is very personal for me, but I think the only way we can learn anything about the deeper meaning of the world around us is to share those scary, dark parts of ourselves. So tonight, allow me to do just that. I will be reading for you "The Grim Gardener." Enjoy. If you need to cry, please do so openly. This is a safe space.

[LIZ *takes a deep breath. "Center yourself," she tells herself, "and read this like it's the most difficult thing that's ever happened in your entire life."*]

There was something beautiful growing here
It was small and good
But I left it alone for far too long
I am not meant to be a gardener.

And so you shriveled
Black. Hard.
It was *my* hand that did it.
I carried the sickle instead of the shovel.

Now the space where you lived stays empty.
I navigate around it as if you were still there.
You were the only one I ever had.
The only chia herb garden I ever had is dead.

I shouldn't have gone on vacation over winter break.
I should have stayed and made sure you were watered.
You were so young. You needed so much.
But I was selfish and really busy during the month of January.

Basil, chives, cilantro, dill.
Had I paid attention to you, we could have had it all.
Mexican food, pasta sauce, whatever.
But instead I went to Florida with my parents and watched
Netflix on my laptop.

You were all I ever needed.
But I killed you before we even had a chance.
Your windowsill stays empty as a memorial to what could have been.
The spice rack tastes like ashes.

[LIZ *takes another deep breath. Maybe wipes away some tears. Now she comes back to the "real world."*]

Thank you. Thank you, but I'm no hero. I'm just a girl speaking her truth. This performance is dedicated to the victims of global warming. Please come to environmental club this week. Thank you. Namaste.

[LIZ *puts her hands together and bows.*]

Didn't Get It

Kate Huffman

FELICIA, 16 to 18

FELICIA *is talking to a friend at her high school.*

NOTE: It's tempting to play FELICIA as super bitter from the beginning, but the piece works better if she's sincerely trying to fight off her negative emotions—until the very end, when she's finally earned her outrage and hurt.

[FELICIA *is smiling as much as is possible.*]

FELICIA   Well, I didn't get it! And that's okay. Really. It's okay. I didn't need to play Juliet. So what if it is my senior year, my final year, the LAST SHOW of my high school theatrical career? So what if I've put in three and a half years of playing townsperson #7 or the drunken old man in *Guys and Dolls*? So what if everyone in the entire theater department KNEW—the moment he picked the play—that it would be me? So what if they were so sure that I'd finally get my turn that people were congratulating me before they even looked at the cast list? And so what if I had to look at them with a SMILE and say, "Oh no, I didn't get it. ASHLEY did."

Ashley. Ashley Larond.

The super popular basketball star, Ashley Larond. Who walked into the auditions on a *lark* because she injured her knee and can't play this season. Wasn't even planning to audition, but happened to be hanging out outside the auditorium that day and thought, "Why not? Wouldn't this be a kick!" Walked in and GOT THE PART.

[FELICIA *is really trying to convince both the audience and herself.*]

And you know what, that's great. Isn't that fun? It's fun, isn't it! And I know why Mr. Fox did it. He, oh, he LOVES surprises! He loves making INTERESTING choices that defy expectations. What a surprise for everyone, isn't it fun? Oh, and there's also the fact that she'll pack the house! All those sports kids—who don't give a rat's ass about theater—will finally come see a play. That will be SO FUN!

And hey, I've got Lady Montague! Lady Montague—that's fantastic. Not Lady Capulet, mind you, who actually has a meaty scene with Juliet, but Lady Montague. The one with two lines up top and then a suicide scene—OFF STAGE. Oh, but you know what we're doing? We're not having her kill herself. We're having her come back onstage at the end, take one of Mr. Montague's lines, and throw herself weeping on Romeo's body. Gee? I wonder why Mr. Fox took it upon himself to rewrite Shakespeare for absolutely no liturgical purpose? Could it be because he feels GUILTY about letting Ashley Larond publicly butcher iambic pentameter while giving me, someone who has put hours and hours and hours of her life into this place—her blood, her sweat, her HEART—YET ANOTHER two-line part????!!!

[*She takes a deep breath.*]

NO, I'm sure that's not it . . . Now if you'll excuse me. I'm going to congratulate Ashley, drop out of the play, and go to basketball tryouts. Why not? Wouldn't that be a KICK!

Pants No More

Kim Currier

KRYSTAL KAMINSKY, 17

KRYSTAL KAMINSKY *stands in a department store dressing room, surrounded by pants. As she tries one pair on, she struggles and falls over. Frustrated, she exits in her shirt and underwear and begins to shout to the people nearby.*

KRYSTAL   Excuse me everyone, I have an announcement to make. I'm sure most of you know this, but wearing pants is the absolute worst! Just to be clear, I hate all types of material. Pants are uncomfortable, confining, and constricting! They're never the right size and they're always too long or too short. If you have any shape at all, you can't get them to fit your waist and hips—it's either one or the other.

Naturally, the size you wear changes with each store and brand, so not only do you have to go through the gruesome process of figuring out which ones actually fit you, but you get to do it again and again for the rest of your life.

Of course, once you've found that magic pair of pants that fit you oh so perfectly, they discontinue them and you have to start your search all over again. Just when you think it can't get any worse, tragedy strikes. The styles have changed and it's no longer socially acceptable to wear them anymore. Before you know it, stores will stop selling them because very few are buying them.

Don't they know you're the one who doesn't care about what society thinks?! Sure you can wear that one magic pair for the time being, but there will come a day when you've worn them too much and that rip is no longer tiny. Before you know it, they've fallen apart before your very eyes.

It will be a sad day and you should mourn properly, but you'll have to move on. The new, awful pair of pants won't really fit you right and you'll hate them. It's okay—we've all been there. It's just how the world works. My point is, get it together designers! This has been a problem for far too long and until you solve this, I'm sticking with dresses!

And no, Mom, it's not because Michael from my English class said he likes it when girls wear dresses—it's because I want to! Feminists don't only wear pants, you know!

The Book Report

Carrie Poppy

CLARA, 14

CLARA *is not a good student. She is panicking because she has been called to the front of the class to give a book report but hasn't read the book, which she now holds.*

CLARA   All right! My turn for the ol' book report! Okay! Perfect. That's perfect because I DEFINITELY read this book. [*She pats the book.*] I definitely read . . . [*She can't think of the title, glances down at the front, and says:*] *The Scarlet Letter*! I absolutely read this and, wow, I loved it. Just . . . really good stuff here. I mean, if I could write this myself, I'd be . . . Whoooo, boy! Just . . . so proud. I would be proud of myself, and . . . Proud.

[*Her teacher interrupts. CLARA listens.*]

Yes . . . Sorry, Mrs. Allen, I just got carried away. So, as far as like, what the book is technically about . . . It's actually, when you think about it, the story of all life. Because every story is in some sense about all life. Who agrees?

[CLARA *raises her hand to indicate that the students should raise their hands to agree. She is stalling.*]

No one? No one agrees? Wow, okay, bunch of misanthropes.

[*The teacher interrupts her again, and* CLARA *responds quickly this time:*]

Okay, okay! I'm sorry, Mrs. Allen. So, about the story. The story is about a very . . . a very . . . red . . . letter. And a very [*She steals a glance at the book's cover.*] . . . And a very bonneted lady. The lady wears a bonnet, WHOOOOO, all the time! And she is a Puritan, I think. Or if not, a wearer of Puritan "garb." That means clothes. [CLARA *winks at the teacher, proud of herself.*] Now, she has a child, a child who also looks to the side. Ummmm . . . [*Looking at book quickly.*] The lady would wear an A on her shirt, [*Realizing it.*] which is why this is called *The Scarlet Letter*!

[*Smug, proud of herself.*]

Yes! That is why they called it that, and why I now call it that, as I present it to you . . . My classmates, colleagues, and friends. [*She's stalling again.*]. Well, that's my report.

[*She listens to Mrs. Allen.*]

Oh, what does the *A stand* for? Well, it's . . . I'm sorry, you said the *A*?

[*Teacher responds "Yes."*]

Well, the *A* stands for . . . "Apple."

[*She sees her teacher shake her head.*]

"Abner."

[*She sees her teacher shake her head.*]

"Advil"?

[*She sees her teacher shake her head.*]

"Anchor"!

[*She sees her teacher shake her head.*]

"Afton"!

[*She sees her teacher shake her head, starts to speed up.*]

"Alexander"! "Angus"! "Albuquerque"!

[*She's going lightning speed now—as fast as is humanly possible.*]

"Arms"! "Amiable"! "Anachronym"! "Antediluvian"! "Acrid," "acid," "actor"! "Abra Cadabra"! "Antonym"! "Artichoke"! "Aardvark"! "Alien"! "Arthouse"! "Actuary"! "Aviary"! "Al-dente"! "A la mode"! "Annie"! "Agnes"! "Anne"! "Annabelle"! "Astrid"! "Albatross"! "Arthur"! "Aaron"! "Art"! "Albert"! "Andrew"! "Anderson"! Alouicious"! "Anton"! "Apricot"! "Anchovy"! "Almond"!

[*Falls to her knees and screams, drawing it out:*]

"AAAAAAAAAAANNNNNNNNNNNNNNGGGGGE EEEEEEEELLLLLLL FFFFFFOOOOOOOOOOOD CAAAAAAAAAAAAAAKE"!

[*There is silence; she sits there, defeated. After a long pause, she springs to her feet, and brightly says:*]

Any questions?

Communal Living

Leah Mann

CLOVER HONEY, 16

Acolyte CLOVER HONEY—*a smart, plain 16-year-old, supplicates herself at the feet of her guru, Father Riverfall. She wears a homespun dirty robe and no shoes.*

CLOVER HONEY   Father Riverfall, I was wondering if, well, I'm not sure how to say this without sounding ungrateful because my heart is full of love . . . but I'd like to go back home. To my other home. Not that this isn't home!

[*Beat.*]

This journey has been amazing and you have changed my life, but the thing is, I'm only sixteen and my decision to run away from my family to live off the grid on a communal farm in Vermont back in January may have been, in retrospect, a bit rash.

[*Beat.*]

Not that I regret anything! I live in the moment. The universe is a vast and beautiful ocean and the tides washed me upon your shore, which has done nothing but enrich me, and now it's time for my journey to continue—at my parent's house, with heat and bathrooms and allergy medication.

[*Beat.*]

Anyway, if I can just have my wallet, driver's license, and phone and my glasses back, that'd be great . . . Oh, and pants, if there are any hanging around, because I'm not sure the robe is going to travel well—probably better to leave it here for a new acolyte to wear.

[*Beat.*]

I did NOT realize that everything we came with was broken down and repurposed towards a more meaningful existence . . . so my glasses are a wind chime now, bringing the music of the air to life?

[*Beat.*]

Then I guess I'll just be going without my identity or clothes or eyesight. What's identity, really? It's like you said, we are all animal bodies with bright lights in our souls waiting to shine, roaming this world as we eat and sleep and love.

[*Beat.*]

I promise I'm not being impulsive. I've been thinking about this for weeks, months—well, two years, seven months, and thirteen days, to be exact. I remember, because I started marking off the days on the wall of my yurt after my parents tried to take me home, but you kept their visit a secret and lied to me.

[*Beat.*]

Which was the right decision on your part! Because I would have left with them and wouldn't have become the strong, independent, intuitive creature you've molded me into. Plus all the things I've learned: cooking, cleaning, building, farming, sewing, pottery, midwifery, butchery, woodworking, leather tanning, irrigation, soap making . . . how to be silent and still, how to respect my elders and serve a greater good . . . All super wonderful life skills that I would never have been forced to learn without your intervention.

[*Beat.*]

That said, I think I'm different from the other girls. They like rubbing your feet and honestly, yeah, it brings me joy to bring you comfort—but it also kind of grosses me out. You have corns and don't wear shoes, so your feet feel like sandpaper sometimes and that nail fungus gets *so* bad in the summer.

I'd like to try deodorant too—I know body odors are natural, but I sweat so much when I'm in the fields during harvest time and I'm not sure mother earth wants me to be smelly and sweaty ALL the time. The other girls are sooo happy writing odes and songs about your wisdom and kindness, but part of me . . . well, part of me would like to write about other stuff—no offense.

[*Beat.*]

Sure, I'll miss sleeping with five other girls huddled up on the floor to stay warm in the winter when I'm stretched out under a comforter on my queen-sized bed. I'll miss the big meals followed by two hours of scrubbing dishes by hand in the river and collecting piles of dung to use as fertilizer, but I would not be staying true to your legacy of honoring our unique spirits if I ignored this call to return to my home.

[*Beat.*]

After lunch? I guess I can wait until after. You're right, I don't want to hit the road hungry . . . of course . . . I wouldn't leave Lydia with all the cleanup—that would be inconsiderate. After lunch and cleanup, then I'll go, with your blessing?

[*Beat.*]

I forgot it was pickling day. I'm not personally much of a pickle person, but yeah, it's a nice gift—I wouldn't want to show up at my parents' house for the first time in three years empty-handed. You always say it's important to show the gratitude we carry in our hearts through the things we give with our hands.

[*Beat.*]

After lunch and cleanup and pickling, then you'll give me your blessing?

[*Beat.*]

Your birthday is tomorrow?

Sweaty-Pits Patsy

Liz Kenny

PATSY LECHNER, 12 to 15

PATSY LECHNER *is looking into a mirror in the girls' bathroom at school.*

PATSY   Oh my god. What is happening to me?

[PATSY *looks at her armpits.*]

Why are my armpits so sweaty?

I wasn't in gym class. I was just sitting in math.

And now there are these huge sweat marks under each of my armpits.

They are the size of an orange.

No. A grapefruit.

Why is this happening to me?

I'm not even hot.

I must be some kind of monster . . . who will sweat for the rest of her life.

I'm a freak.

This doesn't happen to anyone else. I've never even seen Sarah or Lindsay or Becca sweat. Not even sprinting the mile.

They're gonna call me Sweaty Patsy. Sweaty-Pits Patsy.

[*She sings, sadly.*]

"Here she comes.
Sliding down the hall.
With swimming pools for armpits.
It's Sweaty-Pits Patsy."

[*She goes back to speaking.*]

It's gonna be so catchy. Girls are so mean.

[PATSY *looks in the mirror.*]

Oh my god. It's getting worse!

I've gotta make it stop.

Okay. Okay. I'm gonna stuff some paper towels in there.

[*She rushes to the paper-towel dispenser, pulls paper towels out, and stuffs them in her shirt under her armpits.*]

Ooh. That feels good. The towels are absorbing some of the moisture.

[*Beat.*]

I can't let anyone see these sweat marks though.

That's fine. I just won't raise my arms. Ever.

Ugh. But participation counts for 10 percent of my grade.

Ooh! I'll use the old hand drier to dry my pits out.

[PATSY *rushes over to the drier, turns the nozzle up, pushes the button, and holds one pit over the blower. Sings over the blower.*]

I'm dryin' out my armpits.
They're gonna be so dry.

[*She switches pits on the blower, still singing.*]

Patsy! Has such cool and dry pits"—

[*She is interrupted by the sound of the door opening.*]

Oh hello, Mrs. Meyer.

[*Beat.*]

Yes. I have been in here a while.

[*Beat.*]

Yup. Will get straight to class.

[PATSY *looks at herself in the mirror.*]

Okay. Patsy. Time to put your best pit forward.

[*She looks at each pit, which are both still bad, wrinkles her nose, then squeezes her arms in unnaturally tightly, wrinkles her nose again, and walks out.*]

Coolest Thing You Have Ever Seen

Dana Weddle

DEEDEE, 15 to 17

In a hotel room at a ski lodge. The time is 5:00 in the afternoon.

DEEDEE   Kelly, what do you mean, how do I feel? How would YOU feel? I'm MORTIFIED! I could absolutely DIE right now. DIE! Please, somebody just put me out of my misery. My wrist? Oh, I mean, my wrist hurts a little, I guess . . . But my pride, Kelly! My dignity? It's back on that mountain. I'm never leaving this hotel room ever again. What? Yes, I promise. No, my wrist is fine. Yeah, but it's just a small cast. I only have to wear it for a couple of weeks. Kelly, are you even listening to me? Do you even realize what just happened?

Kelly, I FELL OFF THE SKI LIFT. In front of Grant, Kelly. I FELL OFF. STRAIGHT OFF. [DEEDEE *makes a slipping motion.*] *WHOOP!* Off. Who falls off a ski lift? Who falls off a ski lift right next to the guy that is just about to ask them to prom?! Oh my god . . . I must have looked like a total idiot! My life would be so much better right now if I had just impaled myself with my ski pole upon impact. I guarantee you I will never live through this. NEVER. One second we were sitting next to each other, laughing about the prom theme—by the way, "Under the Sea"? Who decided that? Like the Little Mermaid? What is this, our *parents'* prom? Anyway, I was like, "Well, you're student council pres, why don't you use your power and change it, [DEEDEE *whispers like Marilyn Monroe.*] *Mister Presi—whoooooooaaa . . . !*" Then, BAM! Face-planted in the snow twenty feet below. It was awful! The WORST part is, he was *just about to ask me to prom!* I could FEEL it! HE brought up the subject of prom. It was the classic casual conversation ramp-up to the big finish. And man, was there ever a big finish [*Facepalm.*]. UGH. Oh, but the worst part wasn't even falling off the lift. As if that wasn't humiliating enough, after I fell he skied down to me. I tried to play it off, smiled coyly and said, "Wasn't that the coolest thing you've ever seen?" But all I could see was the horror on his face. He couldn't even speak. I started to realize something was terribly wrong. The more I smiled and joked, the more he winced and looked like maybe he was going to throw up. Kelly, MY NOSE WAS BLEEDING all over the place and I had NO IDEA! I was bleeding into my mouth and my teeth were covered in blood. I was too numb from the cold *and* the shock from being *such an idiot* that I had absolutely no idea I looked like some kind of crazy ski zombie feasting on human brains there in the snow on the side of a mountain with blood all over my teeth! It was the most hideous thing that he had ever seen, it was totally obvious! What am I gonna do?

[DEEDEE *freezes.*]

Is that the door? Is someone knocking?

Come in! Oh. Hi. [*She adjusts her shoulders and sits up straight.*] Grant, hello. Yeah, I'm okay. Oh, my wrist? My wrist is fine. Oh, this thing. [*Holds up her arm cast.*] Oh, no, they gave me this to fight off the zombies. [*Swipes arm as if to fight off zombie.*] Ha-ha . . . yeah, the zombies . . . Do you watch *Walking Dead*? No, it's—um . . . oh, never mind. What's that? You were going to

ask me something? [*Falsely bewildered.*] Oh—oh no, I had no idea
you wanted to ask some questions . . . to me . . . about
anything . . . of any kind. What a surprise. [*Her face falls.*] What?
Do I know if who? Do I know if JODI has a date to prom?
Jodi—weirdo, animal-rights Jodi? Jodi-protest-every-science-
experiment-ever, Jodi? Um, HOW would I know? Uh, yeah, she
was my science partner for a hot minute, but we didn't talk about
stupid stuff like PROM. Here's an idea, *Grant*. Why don't you go
ask her your*self*. If you wanted to go to prom with her, you should
have just grown the cojones to go ask her *to her face* a long time
ago! Prom is next Saturday, Grant—only idiots wait 'til the week
before to get a date. Good luck with that. Now please, get outta
my room—I have to elevate my wrist!

Pink Dress

Marisol Medina

CAMI, 17

CAMI, *a 17-year-old high school senior, is a wannabe popular girl—just cute enough to not be seen as a dork but not confident enough to be popular. She's visiting her best friend, Alicia, late one night, with a pink dress in hopes of turning that all around.*

CAMI   Alicia, come on! You have to wear this dress with me to prom. Imagine how cool it will look when we show up in the same pink dress! Everybody will be like, "Oh my god—they're wearing the same dress! How embarrassing!" But then they'll see it's us and go, "Oh yeah, Alicia and Cami always wear the same clothes and the same colors. How cool!" We'll then definitely get into the yearbook when we look all happy that we look the same and, BONUS, we'll get another photo for our yearly besties photo album!

What's the matter with this dress? You don't like pink? [*Confused.*] I've always liked pink . . . why would that be a problem for you now? Well yeah, we always wear what I want us to wear—so what? Yeah, and I take a lot of time to find cool things for us to do, like getting you to drive us to Disneyland and getting you to buy us some Sephora makeovers for Halloween—I think those are pretty cool. [CAMI *is frustrated but tries to clarify the situation.*] Just because I don't want to do anything you want to do has nothing to do with how I feel about you. We're best friends.

Fine, fine, fine! We'll go wherever you want to go to. Where do you want to go? Do you even know where you want to go? Spoken word festival? Like, "Sun. Moon. I make . . . funny noises . . . when I sssspeeeeaaaaak." What would we do, just listen and pretend we care? [*She rolls her eyes.*] I guess that could be fun. Fine! I'll do open mic, poetry slam, or spoken word or whatever. When is it? This Saturday? It had better be before the concert.

We don't have tickets?! You never bought our tickets to Taylor Swift?!!! [*Yelling mad!*] Do you know how many times I called you to remind you to get them?! I kept it in my calendar! Like when the tickets were going on sale, where you had to buy them, what seats I wanted . . . YOU WERE SUPPOSED TO BUY THEM!

You don't like Taylor Swift?! Who are you?!

[*Some boots in a corner suddenly catch* CAMI'*s eye for the first time.*] Oh my god—are those combat boots?! Did you just raid Hot Topic at the mall this weekend and not let me know? [*She looks on the walls as if she never noticed before.*] Why are all your movie posters in French?! When did this happen?! [CAMI *looks horrified as she scans the floor and Alicia's bed.*] There are books everywhere! You READ?!

[*The severity of the moment has just hit her.*]

Oh my god . . . I'm never going to get into the yearbook. You're never gonna wear that pink dress, are you? I can't believe I wasted my friendship on you. After everything I did for you. Fine, I didn't do anything, but I made you DO THINGS! I made you look cool! Thanks to me you knew what to wear! I obviously gave you enough sense to not let anyone know until now that you have a poster of [*She murders the pronunciation.*] "A Bout De Souffle?!"

Is this really where you want to go, Alicia? Be your own person, wear whatever you want, and not have a best friend? Because that's what you're telling me. You're actions right now are ending our digital Friends Forever photo album at page 52.

Fine. Then wear your combat boots and your all-black ensemble to prom. I'm going to wear my fabulous pink dress. And I swear to you, Alicia, before prom I'll find another—a better—best friend to wear this pink dress I got you to buy for yourself . . . and I WILL get into the yearbook.

[CAMI *storms out.*]

Glazed Over

Joanna Castle Miller

DEVRON, 17

DEVRON *is at a birthday party for a favorite member of the popular crowd. She holds up her smartphone.*

DEVRON   Lissa! Smile!

[DEVRON *snaps a photo of Lissa, then taps on her phone.*]

Hmm?

Oh, nothing. I'm just fixing your face.

Don't look at me like that, Lissa. Everybody does it. Look. See? This app scrolls over your face and fixes the double chin and that zit, and makes you look really tan. You're super pale.

Winter, totally not your fault.

There.

This thing is magic. You can load a bunch of photos at once, and it'll show you all your bad posing habits. Like for years I used to smile like this [*Posing.*] and tilt my head like this [*Posing again.*], like I was, I don't know, self-conscious or something. I was kinda fake—but not anymore, because I practiced. And now here's my smile—check it out. [*Posing.*] Natural, right?

I've seen, seriously, probably a 30 to 40 percent increase in Instagram replies since I started using it. People are like, oh my god you're so beautiful, or I get like a hundred likes. And that just makes me more confident, which really comes out in the pictures, you know? It's amazing.

And it's honestly made me a better person in real life, too. Like I push back my shoulders now, which helps prevent that glazed-over expression where it looks like you don't want to be there. You know what I mean. You've had that look in like every picture tonight.

Lissa, I didn't want to say it, but this isn't about me. It's about *you*, and your future. I mean, I've got like all these guys around me all the time now, and, like, I don't know how you and I are gonna ever hang out if you don't work it a little more. *This* [DEVRON *motions at Lissa.*] isn't club material. It isn't Walmart material. Let me see your phone.

[DEVRON *takes Lissa's phone out of her hand.*]

You seem confused. I'm just telling you the truth out of love because I'm, like, your friend.

So here's what I would do, if I were you: I would get the app. Ten dollars. Hashtag worth it! And I'd load like all your photos. And you can edit them like crazy—like whatever, go nuts with it—but then once you start practicing, you'll figure out how to look good all the time, and people will think you're having fun. Because I can tell you, right now? With that expression? People are gonna think you're really sad.

[*Phone notification pings.*]

Yay! There you go! I just went ahead and downloaded it for you. Now . . . smile!

[DEVRON *snaps another photo of Lissa.*]

French Lesson

Angi Lenhart

SOFIA, 13

SOFIA, *smart and focused, is standing behind a barn with Marcus at Tyler's end-of-the-school-year backyard bonfire party.*

[SOFIA *is staring off into a memory, her eyes fixed . . .*]

SOFIA My cousin Carla's quinceañera. That's where I was . . .

[*She slightly snaps out of it.*]

Ya know how people always remember where they were when major events happen in life? When a man first walked on the moon, or someone famous is shot? Well, I was at my cousin's quinceañera when Vicky got french-kissed.

Do you know what I mean? I mean . . . Vicky!! She was the FIRST one of all of us. And it's not that she's not pretty, or that she's a prude, but between the five of us, she wasn't even voted in the top THREE Most Likely to french someone first. I mean, I'm fine that she did—I'm happy for her—but it was just a huge surprise. Especially because she barely knew the guy. They were at day camp together for one week, and BOOM. There's tongue.

So there I was, helping Carla fluff her tulle, and I get this text from Zoe. And she's like "It happened!" Vicky. Frenching at campfire ceremony.

And I was in shock. I was like, shocked! And here it is . . . my cousin's big night, ya know? Her big celebration; and I'm supposed to be there for her, and all I can think about is Vicky, and some guy, and their tongues. It's kind of a big deal.

And I know Carla didn't understand . . . I mean, she's fifteen, so this is old news for her. And I feel bad I had to deal with this right as we're about to light her cake, but what was I supposed to do? We've all been talking about "who would be first" for a long time! And I just, I needed to share the news with someone. It was a major event. Like when Zayn left 1D! You need to talk about it with people, right?

Guys probably don't talk much about kissing, huh?

[*Beat.*]

Well, then, Emily and Zoe didn't waste any time catching up with her. I don't know if you know this, but Emily french-kissed Luis in her basement the very next week, and Zoe claims she frenched a guy at their neighborhood Fourth of July party, but there were no witnesses, so I'm not even sure that's true.

And so that only leaves me and Vanessa. It's not like it's a race, but, I mean . . . we're already behind a lot of the girls here. My sister, Claudia, had it so much easier. She was on city-league soccer her whole life, so she met kids from all over town all the time. She probably started kissing in the third grade! But I'm not in a soccer league. It's not like I meet anyone at my weekend crafty class, and everyone in Bible camp would feel . . . well, you know, it would be weird to hook up there. Do you do any crafting?

[*Beat.*]

Anyway, I really had a good time with you at the Spring Social! I feel like maybe you were going to tell me something before Mrs. Detmer interrupted us. You were talking super close to my face, but . . . I know you're kinda quiet, so maybe it was just so I could hear you. I'm so glad Tyler had this bonfire tonight. Otherwise, I probably wouldn't see you till Fall Festival.

The thing is, Marcus, I just . . . I don't wanna be last. Ya know? I'm always last in my family, and I don't wanna be last of my friends. And I've decided I can't just . . . sit around waiting for things to happen in my life. I mean, I believe in fate, and destiny, but, I'm also ready to move forward. Do know you know I mean?

I'm here. And you're here. And . . . Mrs. Detmer isn't here.

So . . . I just have one question: Peppermint? Or Cinnamon?

Prom

Andra Whipple

ALI, 15 to 18

ALI is talking to David Reece (a supercool boy) in a high school hallway, near the lockers.

ALI   Hello, David. I am here on official business, and that official business is to ask you to prom. Sh-Sh-Sh . . . don't talk yet. I have a lot to say, and if you talk, I'm going to lose my nerve. And it has taken a considerable amount of nerve to get myself over here. I have really worked myself up. I've had six diet cokes, which I know is unhealthy, and probably explains why I have to pee immensely, but I am not going to until I tell you how I feel. I've prepared a speech, so here it goes:

David Reece, I know that girls don't typically ask boys to prom, but I think that is stupid. David Reece, you are so cool. You are a Popsicle personified. David Reece . . . I guess I don't have to say your name every time, do I? Sh-Sh-Sh . . . that was rhetorical. Now is not your time to talk. If you wanted to talk, you should have asked me out yourself. But instead, here I am, so the floor is mine and you have to give it to me. I'm sorry; I guess that was a little rude. I'm just nervous; you'll have to forgive me. You make me feel uncomfortable, in a good way. Man, I really am talking myself into circles, aren't I? You know I'm not a jerk. I'm actually totally lovely, right? Sh-sh-sh, rhetorical. David, come on, you should have picked up on this by now. Oh, man, I really shouldn't have had so many Cokes. That was a super bad move on my part. I feel like my whole insides are about to explode.

But I'm here to talk about you, David! David Reece! I mean, uh, dude. Dude, you are one of the nicest-smelling dudes I have ever smelled. It's like, salty maple syrup combined with a sea breeze and a wood shop. If I knew anyone in the cologne business, I would call them and tell them that they had better show up to Bay Ridge High School and bottle your essence, stat. It would be a best seller. And not just because I would buy several bottles to smell for myself. Wow, that sounded creepy. I'm not a creep; I just appreciate a good scent when I smell one. But I do not just like you for superficial reasons. I know you are more than your smell. But still, smell is pretty important considering that the rest of the boys at our school smell like fried fish. Besides your smell, you are nice too. One time when I dropped my soda in the cafeteria, you gave me yours. And it was a Fanta, which I know is your favorite. So that had to be hard for you, and I think that perfectly exemplifies how selfless and big-hearted you are. Not every person would do that. I know that one time the other guys dared you to put a Kick Me sign on my back, and you didn't do it. This is impressive both because it shows you are not a butthead and it shows that you have a more sophisticated sense of humor than most of the boys in this school. You know that Kick Me is a pretty played-out joke at this point, and I respect that. You're a man that knows comedy. I would say that you're funnier than Eddie Murphy, but I don't want to lie. Eddie Murphy is the best. I think you are a close second, though, so don't get discouraged. It took him years to get as funny as he is.

But you know all of this, so let me tell you some things you don't know about me. I'm awesome. I have a 4.2 GPA. It would be higher, but Mr. Watts didn't understand the extreme merit of my fifty-two-page exposé on *Game of Thrones* and gave me a C minus because he is an animal, and not the good kind. I speak four languages, and yes, three of those are from science-fiction book series, but I know that only makes it cooler because I am not just a lemming who learns French because people told her to. My idea of a perfect date is walking hand in hand through the forest looking for Scincomorpha lizards. They are my favorite kind of lizards, for obvious reasons. Oh, that's not obvious? Well how about the fact that a blue-tongued skink is a member of the Scincomorpha lizard family. I am the captain of the scientific debate team, an accomplishment that is especially exciting considering that most people don't even know the scientific debate team exists. It's very underground, which I'm pretty sure is cool and edgy. I've already made my prom dress, and obviously I made it out of duct tape. What you might not have guessed is that I found duct tape that is blue and glittery. Yes, it is in honor of the blue-tongued skink. I've also made a black leather jacket that says "SKINK" on the back of it. Sometimes people make fun of me for it, but I think that in life you have to stick to your convictions. I play the banjo and I've won a statewide championship for my latest banjo composition, "Scales: A Girl's Tale." I have already been accepted, full ride, early admission to Yale, and I know you have, too. I'm not saying that we have to continue our relationship past prom into college, but you should know that we have the option. That's what I have to offer, and frankly it's a lot. I don't want you to feel intimidated, so let me remind you that I am currently registering romantic interest in you. I have judged you to be worthy of my incredibly high standards.

So, that will be all. I desperately have to pee now, so, David, you may give me your answer on . . . What? The dance was last weekend? Oh. That is. Embarrassing. Much more embarrassing than a Kick Me sign. I guess this could only get worse if I emptied myself of all six Diet Cokes right now in public. And I don't want to do that, so I guess I'll be going now. Unless you want to go look for blue-tongued skinks with me? I know a great place.

One-Hit Confessions

Linda Landeros

TIFFANY, 16

TIFFANY *sits with her two friends, laughing and chitchatting, and is then suddenly overwhelmed with having to break the news . . .*

NOTE: The name of the fictitious band One Way Street can be replaced with the name of an actual band.

TIFFANY   Hey, girls, I, um . . . I have to tell you something. I'm gonna try to get through this without crying, but, um . . . I have no idea who the band One Way Street is! Oh my gosh, I'm so embarrassed! No, I'm being totally serious, this is not a joke! I have been pretending to know who they are when you all talk about them, but I have no clue. I know, I know—I've been nodding along as if I know who you're all talking about—but I have no idea who those guys are. I don't even listen to their songs; I just mumble and move my lips when you all start singing lyrics to their songs, like this: [TIFFANY *lip-synchs mumbo-jumbo lyrics.*] See? You've just never noticed before.

Now, I know what you're thinking. I could easily just Google them, right? But what kind of person would I be if I had to Google every little thing? We cannot let a search engine dictate our access to knowledge! Shouldn't my knowledge come from within? I mean, do you Google what two plus two is? No, because that knowledge comes from here [*She points to her head.*]

and here. [*She points to her heart.*] If you ask me who One Way Street is, I cannot tell you from here [*She points to her head.*] or here. [*She points to her heart.*] So why would it matter what Google says? Well, it doesn't.

So you just have to accept that I don't know who they are, and have been lying about it. I'm not proud of myself for having lied to you all for so long. I feel really bad. But I can tell from your expressions that you're judging me, and that's not cool. Shame on you all! You're supposed to be my friends, through thick and thin. Every group of girls needs a quirky one. Well, I'm your quirky girl now. I'm like the Phoebe and you two are Monica and Rachel. Wait—you haven't watched *Friends*? It's so good!

I mean—shame on you! [*Beat.*] So now what? Where do we go from here? You're probably wondering what else have I lied to you about. Well, I lied about going to Paris last summer with my family. Sort of. I went to Paris, Texas, not Paris, France. My family is from Texas, not France. I lied to you about my cultural background to seem cooler! You all just seemed so cool when you talked about having gone to Europe with your families, and you know how to speak French. So I wanted to fit in. I don't know what Paris is like; I just nodded my head and said random French words like *oui* or *le boeuf* when you all started speaking in French. I have no idea what those words mean.

I also lied about having tried escargot. Those are the frog legs, right? I would never try them. But I said I had to sound cooler. And my favorite food isn't actually sushi. It's tater tots and banana pudding. It's my favorite meal in the whole wide world! I dip the taters in the pudding, and it's amazing! I love it so much but have been so ashamed to admit that's what I eat, so I hide in the bathroom during fourth period every day and eat taters and pudding in secret. It's disgusting, but I didn't think anyone would understand.

I can tell by how you're looking at me that you're weirded out right now. Like, how many more truth bombs am I gonna drop on you all? Well that's it. No! It's chocolate pudding. I said banana because it's cooler than plain ol' chocolate, but I like chocolate pudding. There! I'm done confessing. That's all you need to know about who I truly am. I'm weird, I get it! But you should love me no matter what! [*In tears.*] What? Yes, of course I accept your apology! I love you girls, too!

I'm glad we're past all that. The simple truth is, I don't listen to mainstream pop music at all; it's just not my thing. I've always been afraid to admit this, but I really like listening to one-hit wonders from the nineties. I just think they're so cool; they just do that one song that takes over the nation and then walk away like nothing and go back to being regular people. They don't wait 'til they're overplayed and in rehab or whatever. They make a statement, and disappear. Nothing is cooler than that in my book!

So, I'm telling you all this because I can't be a part of the One Way Street party we were planning. It just wouldn't be right. Plus, I actually had a party planned that night for my One-Hit Wonders of the Nineties fan club. We're having a mixer for others who are new to the group. You're all invited to the party, though. Well, I gotta go—I gotta buy some streamers for the party. [*Puts headphones in and starts singing.*] "I'll be there for you, when the rain starts to fall!" [*Stops singing.*]

You've gotta know that one. Really?! You really just need to watch *Friends*.

Staci's Room Tour Video

Chrissy Swinko

STACI, 13 to 15

STACI is in her bedroom, taping a "room tour" video to post online. She adjusts the camera, fixes her hair and shirt in the monitor, and presses record. She steps back and enthusiastically speaks to the audience as though they were the camera.

STACI   Hi, I'm Staci! Shout-outs to all my subscribers and all my new friends watching this video.

So I got challenged to do a room tour video . . . so here it is!

The first thing you see when you walk into my room is on the door—it's a picture of the Eiffel Tower—because I think it's really cute and I love my French class and learning French.

Cool, and here's my dresser. This is where I keep all my clothes that I don't want to hang in the closet. On top I have some books and school stuff, and all the letters my dad sends me, because he doesn't live here right now.

This part of my wall above the dresser I really love because I put up all these pictures of my friends and my sister and my brother and my mom. It's in kind of like a heart shape and I think it's really cute. This is my countdown calendar for when my dad is coming home—I update it every month.

Here is my closet! Pretty obvious—I keep clothes in here. Here's all my dresses, and other stuff I like to hang up, like my dance costumes. Oh! This is the dress I wore the last time I visited my dad. And yes, as you can see, everything is color coded. So yeah!

Cool, so this is my bed. I have these cute pillows, and this one has a butterfly. I have another Eiffel Tower on this one. I love my pillows and sleeping in!

This is my desk-slash-vanity table. I do homework here and also put on makeup and stuff. It's really cute and my dad painted it blue for me before he went to prison. I really like it, but maybe it would be cool if it was purple and matched my butterfly pillow? He'll be back in like twenty-six months, so maybe he'll paint it again.

Comment below—where do you do your makeup? Comment, and I might shout you out in my next video!

Right next to my desk is my bookcase. Here's all my math books! I love math and numbers. Math is in all kinds of stuff like music and dance. So yeah!

When my dad was home he always helped me with my homework, because he does lots of math at his job. He's really smart, but his friend at work lied and said he did insider trading. But my mom said he totally *didn't*. Haters gonna hate. That's why I never gossip.

Okay. So yeah! Comment below—what's your favorite thing in your room?

Watch the screen 'cause here come last week's shout-outs! Shout-out dance!

[STACI *dances and points as if pointing to the names scrolling across the video.*]

So yeah! Please subscribe and share this video. Love all my subscribers! Love you, Dad! Bye!

We Come in Peace

Derek Heeren

JENNA, 17

JENNA *talks with her boyfriend of 3 months, Caleb, who is also captain of the football team, about sleeping together after prom. JENNA's excited about the idea, but wants to make sure he has all of the facts before doing so, which clearly makes Caleb upset.*

JENNA   You're mad at me.

I don't understand! We talked about this. I told you my family are illegal aliens that came here to make a better life for ourselves and you said you were okay with that. Well, why does it matter that we're *actual* aliens from Magmar 7? I'm still a regular, teenage girl. I like pizza and boys and horses and I get pimples. I'm just from another spiral arm of the galaxy . . . and my pimples are on the inside.

Listen, Caleb, I think we can make this work. I like you. I really do. And you like me. That's what it's about, right? I'm ready to take this to the next level.

Come on, Caleb, this isn't hard. I'm funny, good with conversation, I've got perky breasts, a symmetrical face, an off-the-charts IQ, and I'm willing to sleep with you. Why am I trying to convince *you* on this?

Yes, I'm a Magmarian—so what? Can't you get past that? I've learned to accept that you put mayo on everything. It's not that big of a deal. I just have a lower resting body temperature than you. And I can see into the ultraviolet spectrum. That's not something that's going to come up in our everyday life (unless I see certain shades of yellow—I'm allergic). Oh, and I have some slight . . . ESP, but I promise I won't use it. Unless you'd like me to. I can tell you would not. Okay, noted. Also, I have three hearts, but most of that is related to a gill system that I don't use here on Earth. Sorry, I'm freaking you out. It's not freaky! I'm normal!

Caleb, it's still me. I'm still Jenna. I still want to hook up with you. I just want to be totally honest with you so you're not surprised by what "hooking up" entails. Which, consequently, involves some "hooks" and a "tail" . . . Caleb . . . CALEB!

[*Sigh.*]

[JENNA *holds up her hand, as if it's a sock puppet, then turns it toward herself and addresses it.*]

Ah well, it's okay, Hand Monster. I could tell he wasn't going to go for the whole laying-eggs-in-his-chest thing, anyway. Now we have to start over with someone new. Let's go try Matt—he seems like he's got a nice, juicy chest.

Meeting His Mom

Catherine Nicora

KIMBERLY, 16 to 18

Entryway of a beautiful house.

KIMBERLY   So this is Tommy's house? Cool, cool. Thank you for letting me in—I didn't know Tommy was still at practice. I just think it's always good to get places early and didn't want to just wait outside.

You guys are very clean. And you can see the ocean from the living room? Wow, wow. Even your shag is perfect. That's what I call carpets. You've got sweet shag. I can't believe I'm finally meeting you—do you like me? You are so beautiful and you have Tommy's nose. Tommy is always saying how his mother means so much to him. I thought he was crazy. I mean, my mom only cares about whomever the new boyfriend is that month. I mean, I was really nervous to meet you. And excited.

I started off like, "Oh my gosh, I hope she likes me!" But then I was like, "Well, Tommy likes me, so she'll like me." But then I was like, "What if she doesn't like a single thing about me, not even my hair?" And then I was like, "She better like me! I'm so awesome!"

For example, I'm a dancer! I just started last month—that's when I first hung out with TT (that's what I call him) and so I've just been so motivated to dance! You know! Dance like no one's watching but with the hope someone's watching and they like it.

He's a really good dancer. Very hot. I can't believe I just said that to his mom. But you're cool. Cool, cool.

But anyway, we've been hanging out a lot, TT and I—like our first kiss was crazy tongue session—it was like my world was exploding and . . . wow. We've been seeing each other every day. His smile on campus makes me so motivated to go to class! Will he see me in my new outfit? Does he like my ponytail? MMM.

You know what I love about TT? I can't believe I just said that, but I have to be honest—I love him, and what I love most is that he just really cares and really sees me. It feels special; I feel alive.

He's been hanging out with me a lot one-on-one. When he took me hiking after school last Friday he held my hand so gently and told me he's never felt this way with anyone else. I thought we were just going on a hike, the most beautiful hike, on top of the hill I don't know its name, but we called it our hill and you can see the whole city, even the dump, which we thought was funny, and it was the first time I ever had like real sex—full on—and it felt so good and . . . c-can can I take that last part back? I didn't mean to say that. I um. We just kissed and got carried away. Do you not like me?

My mind's going crazy 'cause it's my first time and are we going to get married? Does he really love me?

I'm not what you think I am; I'm really sweet and lovely and I would like to start over. I'm just so nervous, can you tell? I should have waited outside. Or I should have told you about our first date. It was great. We got ice cream. It was nice.

Should I go? Should I stay?

You're not his mom?!! You're the cleaning lady?

Wait. Really?

Wow, wow. Thank you. I'll just sit down and wait.

Boo-Hoo First Born

Moreen Littrell

AVA, 13 to 16

AVA *is speaking to the salesperson at Sephora while testing perfumes.*

AVA   Do you have any perfume that Cinderella would wear?

Have I seen Cinderella? Uhh, yeah-ah, like three times. My friends and I call her "second-class-citizen Cindy." [*Sigh.*] Poor Cindy. I know how she feels. Why??? Because I have one sister who is older, which makes me the baby of the family. BUT apparently my mom didn't get the MEMO . . . because instead of babying me, she always has this extra empathy for . . . [AVA *bows as if to the Queen.*] the First Born.

She'll say, "Oh, Megan is soooo busy. Poor thing. Just runs herself ragged. You should help her with her chores, since you're not doing anything."

I'm like, "Umm yeah, poor Megan—she ran herself ragged running from the cops last night through a rose bush so she wouldn't get caught for underage drinking. If not for her daily B12 shots, I don't know how she'd get through the day. It took her two hours to pick out her wardrobe for school tomorrow. Choosing between *indigo* blue jeans and *faded* blue jeans can really be taxing. Especially after four hours of selfies and three hours on the phone with Dan. Yeah, poor Megan, if only Quarterback Dan would just text, she wouldn't be straining her voice so much and have that poor raspiness. Yeah, boo-hoo Megan, she has a sexy voice."

But I don't get into the histrionics with my mother. She's already under so much stress. She quit smoking two weeks ago. So we are all being "extra sensitive." Except of course she *didn't* quit smoking. But we're all supposed to pretend like the garage doesn't smell like an ashtray that hasn't been dumped in ten years. I can smell it a mile away. I mean, seriously, does she think I'm pulling my shirt up over my nose because my chest smells so good? It . . . does . . . actually. My décolletage smells ravenous compared to *Marlboro*. But now? [*Smells under shirt.*] My virgin skin smells of [*Waves the air to her nose.*] . . . Ivory soap . . . with notes of . . . ammonia, carbon monoxide, and methane . . . plus sixty-six more cancer-causing ingredients . . . topped off with lavender and rosemary oil. Yep, smokers can get cancer AND essential oils all in one. Did you know that? We learned that last year in Mr. Osterman's class. [*A beat.*] Do you think the same chemist who made cigarettes made this? [*Holds up cologne.*] Drakkar Noir? No? Hmmm.

Anyway, tonight my mom's going to ask me to help Megan with the dishes so that Megan can study for her French 1–2 final. But I'm going to say, "I'm sorry, I'd really love to help the First Born communicate in some language other than emoticons, but I'm starting to really care about how I look now . . . and smell . . . so that's really going to cut into my 'help poor Megan' and 'pretend my mom doesn't smoke' time."

Plus it's my birthday. So there's *that*. That's why I am here. I need more perfume test strips. Maybe I'll try Marc Jacobs Daisy or Prada Candy this time. I just know I need something stronger than Flowerbomb to neutralize "Smoky the Mo."

Mormon Wife

Alessandra Rizzotti

MARIANNE, 16

MARIANNE *is a boring, naive girl who just wants to fall in love, with anyone, even if he sucks. She modifies her desires and wants any guy who shows interest. Her fiancé is Mormon, so she's converting and has accepted his other wives, even though it feels inappropriate to her, deep inside.*

MARIANNE   Mom, you know how I never grew up with any sisters? You know how I always used to pretend my Barbies and My Little Ponies were like my family? I'm so excited because, guess what? Bradley proposed to me to be his third wife, received by way of the Lord's guidance. Now I'll have sisters AND I'll be the favorite for a while because I'm the youngest! Hee-hee.

I see this as a chance to serve God and I just don't think there's any reason to go to college anymore, Mama. I really don't. I know I thought I'd do design or something for interiors, but now I just want to have children and be of service to this new family I'll be creating. Good thing I've been on the track team so long! My legs are toned and ready! My hips probably need to get ready for birthing, though, so I'll start eating more or something! Eeeee!

Please accept this news with love and know that I've prayed so much that I know in my heart and soul, it is my path. I know you've never been a fan of men with multiple ladies and all, since daddy cheated, but this is like the rules from God, so it's not scandalous or anything. Plus, we help each other out and stuff. We're all supposed to be one big family.

Have you accepted God the way I have, Mama? Sometimes I wonder with you. You read so much of that nonsense about self-love that I just don't know if you're right in the head. Don't take that as offense or anything—I just feel so wise the way I've been living recently that I just can't see any other way. I'm not judging you . . . I just feel a little distant from you, and I would prefer not to, which is why I would love it if you walked me down the aisle, please—especially now with Daddy gone and all?

And if you don't mind, I'd love for you to help me plan the wedding shower and host it too. And perhaps you can help me with the planning of the night itself? I was thinking a forest theme or something with music from *Into the Woods*, maybe with fairies for the centerpieces. I know I haven't done much in the way of event organizing and your expertise would be much appreciated, since you used to wrap presents at Robinsons-May and all. I swear I think this could make our mother-daughter relationship a lot stronger. I won't go Bridezilla on you or anything. LOL.

What? No, his other wives wouldn't plan the wedding. They're the bridesmaids, but they only help with raising babies. Maybe I should ask. There should be a sister-wife guidebook for Mormons or something. I was thinkin' of getting in a sister-wife support group just to get some better insight. It's all new stuff. Taking the Mormon pledge has felt like an awakening in itself, but this wife thing is all-new territory.

I love you, Mama, just like God loves you. And I would hope we can make this marriage, this family, and this new life even more full of love than ever before. And when I get jealous of the other wives, I'll need to talk to someone, Mama, and I hope it can be you, promise? Now, what do you think: wedding DJ, or choir? I was even thinking we could make the table place settings like vintage or something—maybe with a Rainbow Bright or Lisa Frank or Carebear theme—so maybe the DJ is better, but he will only play really vintage '80s music. I want color in my wedding, too. And I was thinking, you know how my girls love Trapper Keepers? We could do Trapper Keepers as gifts with Hello Kitty doodads or something. Just an idea. I was thinking I want my shoes and dress to be SUPER sparkly princess status. So what do you think?

[*She stares at her mom.*]

You don't like it. Mama, I'm doing it for the Lord! Accept the ideas that are coming through me by way of the Lord's love.

[*She bows her head, closes her eyes, and prays. Then she opens her eyes and stares at her mother.*]

Don't worry about me. I'll have six sisters by the time I'm eighteen. THEY'LL take care of me.

Phone Drone

JP Karliak

SAM, 13 to 15

SAM *never takes her eyes off her phone, and her mom wants her to pay attention to the world around her. But tonight before dinner, SAM's mom will learn just how aware of the world SAM is.*

SAM   Just one second.

Just one second, okay?

Mom, with all due respect, there are, in fact, things I could be doing more important than whatever you have to say. I know that's a crushing blow to your ego; I don't mean it to be. I'm just saying that governments rise and fall every day regardless of whether we discuss my math homework.

[SAM *resumes texting.*]

No, I didn't say I'm responsible for government upheaval . . . that'd be crazy, right? . . . I'm just pointing out where our predinner check-in falls on the scale of importance. Not to mention, why can't we talk during dinner like everyone else does? Honestly, I don't mind if you talk with your mouth full.

I can't tell you what I'm doing.

Because I can't.

You can't ground me for that—I have the right to remain silent. Okay, okay, fine—the reason is . . . it's classified.

From who? From everybody, not just you. Wow, your ego is massive, isn't it? Look, there's no reason to panic. When I say "classified," I just mean it's something very important, but completely and utterly harmless.

[*Mom takes the phone.*]

No! A million people will die! I'm serious! And not because I kill them. Because I can't save them from imminent, instantaneous destruction unless you give me back my phone.

Yes, "harmless" was a gross understatement! Mom. Please. This is not time to assert your parental power. You have to trust me. Your child. Your flesh and blood, your legacy embodied, the fruit of your good example. You can trust your own child, can't you? Mama?

I don't know who dinged the car door! The phone, Mother. Now!

Okay, fine. Fine. Just know that by saying this now, I'm breaking multiple laws, and I can't guarantee your safety or the safety of this family: I'm a spy. Yes, a spy. Okay, I recognize it's hard to believe, but I don't think it's funny. Especially not that funny. Please stop laughing.

All right, you want proof? No problem, I'll try to keep this to a minute or less since a million might be dead by then, but here we go:

You and Dad are always on me for too much time on my phone, but every second I spend on it is to protect the life, liberty, and happiness of the American people. Every text is an encoded message with the FBI, CIA, NSA, Homeland Security, and now and then, even the president. Every tweet, an encrypted instruction to operatives overseas. Every selfie, a facial recognition scan to access the government's most restricted databases. You think I'm ignoring you listening to indie rock? I'm listening to wiretaps from Beijing. You think I'm launching birds at pigs, I'm launching drone strikes at chemical weapons plants. You think I'm posting my status to Facebook? I'm not. Nobody posts on Facebook anymore.

With every allegedly superficial swipe of who's hot and who's not, I'm actually judging which soldiers are best equipped for a black ops mission. The last time I favorited someone's pic, they got a Congressional Medal of Honor.

Bottom line is that there is too much danger in this world to entrust heroics to every mid-'20s cadet fresh out of Langley and West Point. Younger, faster, smarter minds are required to keep the cogs and wheels turning in the complex game of espionage, and I stepped up to the challenge. Believe me, it's not easy facing your parents' constant criticism and disdain, fearing any day you guys might write me off as "our kid who we're pretty sure will live at home long after high school," but that's a risk I'm willing to take if it means you and Dad can sleep safely one more night in a world teetering on the edge.

Now if that sounds more important than my day at school, I'd appreciate you giving me back my phone so I can send a text that will mean hundreds of thousands of other mothers and fathers will survive the night, too. No big deal.

[*Gets the phone back.*]

Thanks, Mom. Yeah, we'll talk during dinner.

[*Finishes texting. The phone rings. Looks around before answering.*]

Did you receive the transmission?

I know! His butt is amazing!!

Change Is Constant

Leah Mann

MIA, 16

MIA *is a tomboyish teen with several piercings running up her ear and wearing baggy pants and an old men's sweater. She faces off with her parents in the entrance of their house. She has just returned from a music festival in the desert with her best friend, Greta.*

MIA   Okay, so yes, I got my ear pierced . . . I mean, it WAS already pierced—I just pierced it more, which should totally not be a big deal. You SAID it was okay and I asked. You guys are such great parents and so understanding, I knew it'd be okay but I asked anyways, out of respect.

[*Beat.*]

And yeah, maybe I had already gotten it pierced when I called you and "asked permission," but you said, and I quote, "We'd prefer if you didn't, but you're halfway across the world and can't stop you." Some people got their noses and belly buttons done, so a few earrings . . .

[*Beat.*]

Ugh, fine, SEVEN isn't a few, if we're getting technical about it; either way, seven earrings that are limited to my ears isn't even that punk rock. It's normal now. Greta got eight and her parents didn't freak.

[*Beat.*]

Seriously? I do NOT do everything that Greta does. How could you say that? She's on the softball team, for one thing, and I hate team sports; plus, she wears super girlie clothes, which I don't do. You should be GRATEFUL about that, by the way. Tons of the girls at school wear totally slutty stuff to school, but not me. What am I wearing? What am I wearing right now? Huh? . . . Dad's old corduroys and a sweater.

[*Beat.*]

You were NOT looking for these—you never wear these. I found them in the back of your closet under a pile of old shoes.

[*Beat.*]

Your pants are not important. What's important is that I'm growing and this was, like, a ritual that Greta and I went through together. It commemorates our trip and our friendship. I have a life outside of this family, okay? Maybe that makes you guys sad, but change is a constant—it's a rule of the universe—and you have to accept that. I'm not some little kid—I'm sixteen and I have my own thoughts and feelings and goals and style.

[*Beat.*]

I'm not scratching my shoulder.

[*Beat.*]

Fine, I'm scratching because it's itchy because this demure totally respectable sweater I'm wearing is itchy.

[*Beat.*]

I'm wearing this sweater because I'm cold. You know I run cold, it's my body, and yeah, I know it's summer, I'm not DUMB, I just have bad circulation.

[*Beat.*]

You guys need to chill out. I haven't even finished unpacking and you're giving me the sixth degree about stupid stuff like an earring instead of asking what I've seen and how I've grown as a person. I mean, this summer was utterly spiritual and religious and mind opening. I slept in the desert and built houses and saw poverty and talked about God and goodness and faith and the injustice in the world. I saw shooting stars and felt how tiny I am in the universe and made the best friends ever in the world who are beautiful souls. But yeah, let's argue about a few . . . SEVEN . . . earrings and a little tattoo.

[*Beat.*]

Huh? . . . I said seven earrings.

[*Beat.*]

Nope, I don't think I said that.

[*Beat.*]

I won't take the sweater off—I'm cold.

[*Beat.*]

Are you trying to give me hypothermia? I have life skills now and I could survive without you two. I really could. I have a support system outside of the bourgeois, rule-riddled, nuclear family you guys have constructed.

[*Beat.*]

Okay, maybe it's a little dramatic to say I could survive on the streets but will get hypothermia if I take off my sweater, but that's not the point. I was being, metaphorical, or whatever.

[*Sighs.*]

You win. I'll take off the sweater.

[*Beat.*]

See, no big deal. Just a teeny tiny tattoo like a million other people have.

[*Beat.*]

It's small and you can't see it under most shirts . . . yes, Greta got one too.

[*Beat.*]

She's my girlfriend in the way that she's a girl and my friend. More than a friend, she's like my soul mate. She gets me. We don't even have to talk or anything, she just gets me, but NO, she's not my girlfriend in a lesbian way. Not because there's anything wrong with that, and if she WAS my girlfriend you guys should be THRILLED that your daughter was with such a totally awesome and loving, beautiful person.

[*Beat.*]

But she isn't, because I'm not a lesbian—I just like to wear comfortable clothes and jeans are the worst. But wearing Dad's pants doesn't mean I don't like being with boys in . . . you know . . . like, sexually, I guess.

[*Beat.*]

I can't believe we're having this conversation. Tattoos have nothing to do with liking boys or girls. Can we stay on topic for thirty seconds?

[*Beat.*]

It's a compass, just like the one you gave me that used to be Grandpa's. It's so I always know who I am and where I am in the universe, no matter what.

[*Beat.*]

Seriously? You like it?

[*Beat.*]

Mom, jeez, don't cry . . . What, did you think I was going to get, like, a butterfly on my butt or something? I'm not tacky, I'm indie . . . Mooom, you're gonna make me cry, too.

[*Starting to cry.*]

See what you did? I love you guys, like so much, and I wouldn't do anything to my body that I didn't find meaningful and important.

[*Beat.*]

Dad, you better not start too. Of course I love you guys. A tattoo or piercing . . . SEVEN piercings doesn't change that. You guys being cool with who I am just makes me love you more.

[*Wiping away tears and snot.*]

So, can I like, tell you guys the secrets of the universe now that we got all that out of the way, because seriously, I did so much thinking and I'm totally going to blow your minds. Did you know they don't even use toilet paper in a lot of places? They just, like, throw some water on there. I mean, how many trees would we save if we stopped using toilet paper? Can you do the math on that? Hold on, let me get a pencil.

Brace

Alessandra Rizzotti

KITTY, 16

KITTY *sits down, stiff in a neck brace. She's in a support group with fellow Asperger's kids.*

KITTY   Hi, I'm Kitty. I have high-functioning Asperger's. Uh . . . so . . . this week . . . let's see, because of my car accident right before prom (damn Smart cars are so friggin' small), I'm now in this neck brace and people are all like, "Poor Kitty. She'll never get a date to the prom." Well little do they know, last NIGHT, I LOST my virginity! In THIS brace, on the DOUBLE-DECKER prom bus! So, I'm just PROOF that disabled people CAN have fun. It's not like we're robots. I may LOOK like the Terminator, but I freak like Kat von D. Bow chika bow wow!

[KITTY *gets up and sways her hips, getting loud, trying to act sexy. She hurts her neck when doing this.*]

Ow. O-M-G. I think I need to call Dr. Cooper.

[*She sits down, in pain.*]

Ha. Sorry. Whoops. Broke my bottom lines. So sue me! No more sexy moves for me! Anyways, Tommy may have felt bad for me, because of the Asperger's AND the brace, but whatever, he has his own issues like agoraphobia and shit so, I was like a sexual GOLD MINE to him. The thing is, I can't really, you know, spread my legs that well. I think I have nerve damage from the air bag hitting my inner thigh in the accident. That, or pole-fitness class. I do that class for better arm strength and to get comfortable in my body since, you know, we Asperger's kids are NEVER that. I've learned how to be more present or whatever, which might help you guys. Like I actually made EYE CONTACT with the pole—they made us pretend it was a hot guy or something and DUH I made the pole look like Tommy in my mind.

Anyways, not sure if Tommy and I will DO IT again, but I should be out of this brace in a year or so, so my boobs might be bigger by then and then he'll probably LOVE me. We'll see. I'm not like banking on it or anything, but if I bother him enough, he'll do it. He's pretty much a shut-in with Dungeons and Dragons, so I just have to bang on his window long enough and he'll be like, "Sure, I'll do you." He-he.

Well, that's all I got for this week. Sheila, you can go next, if you can TOP ME. Just kidding.

[KITTY *turns her head abruptly to the left, as if someone just made a sigh. She hurts her neck again.*]

Ow. Barbara. I'm not being that mean, FYI. And guys, at least I noticed her doing that eye roll. Progress on my social cues. Five points for me!

[*She does a victory upward fist. She hurts her neck again.*]

Dammit!

Advice from a Babysitter

Keisha Cosand

SHELBY, 13 to 15

SHELBY *is at the park on the swings with her friend, advising her to never start babysitting.*

SHELBY   She asked you to babysit? Girl, I wouldn't do it. I mean, once you start, they never let you go. I'm telling you, I made the mistake of agreeing to babysit for my next-door neighbor, Angelica, last year. Anyways, I'm totally trapped now.

Four years ago, she and her husband, Rob, spawned Chloe. Everyone thinks she is SO sweet. I mean, even I thought she was cute until she learned words.

Why do I watch her? Believe me! I try to say no, and sometimes it works, but my own mom pressures me. "Honey, come on, honey, they're our neighbors . . . What else are you going to do?" Umm, I can think of a THOUSAND things. Then there is Angelica with her big desperate eyes that say, "Please, I'm in a bind. It's just for a few hours." I mean, she does pay bank. Where else am I going to get twenty bucks an hour? True, it's a lot, but I'm not even sure it's worth it. Seriously, watch out. Can't you mow lawns or something? I heard you can sell stuff on Etsy . . . people are so sucker for crap kids make.

The last time I said yes, Angelica opens the door, and Chloe is right behind her—a three-foot puff of pink lace and tulle, plastic glass slippers, and a rhinestone tiara atop her ringlets of carrot-colored hair. This whole princess thing with little kids is scary! I know, right? Little entitled monsters.

Anyway, I say, "Hi, Chloe!" and she says, "I'm not Chloe! I am the 'printheth'!" Her mother smiles and kisses her head and looks at me with an "Isn't she the most adorable thing you have ever seen on this planet?" look. I mimic the smile but want puke Pepto pink vomit to match her frickin' tutu.

Then, Angelica and Rob debrief me on Chloe's dietary and screen-time restrictions: no sugar, artificial colors, or sweeteners, no white flour, and only thirty minutes of Disney Junior. They make a quick exit, and Chloe begins a high-pitched screaming rage. You wouldn't believe the sound that came out of her; it's like Chucky and a banshee had a baby. I literally checked the windows to see if any had shattered.

Believe me, this is not the first time I witnessed such a freak of nature. I have learned to come prepared with emergency supplies. I still don't think you should do it. But if you decide to, this is like the best trick in the book. Just don't get caught, and like make sure the kid doesn't have any real allergies. I think you could probably go to jail if the kid dies from anaphylactic shock or something. Anyway, after what seems like forever but is probably five minutes, she calms to my promises of Kraft Macaroni and Cheese, red Kool-Aid, and Oreo Double Stufs for dinner in front of my old *Sponge Bob: The Movie* DVD. I know I'll totally regret giving her processed sugar and red dye No. 5, and it will exacerbate her evil temper and probably increase her chances of getting ADHD, but it was seriously the only way to get her to shut up and to keep my brain from exploding.

It gets worse. Just let me tell you, it gets worse. Next, she says, "I want to play 'printheth'!" I swear, I feel my body descending toward hell when she demands that I be the "printh." I politely tell her I am a girl, so I cannot be the "printh," but I'll gladly be her fairy godmother (or evil stepmother), and I can use my wand to turn her into different things (like the little toad that she is) and it will be fun. She says, "No! You are the 'printh'! You have to do what I say, or I will tell my mom you gave me Oreos!"

Yeah, I'm a little worried because my mom would be totally pissed if she finds out I raided our cupboard. No, she wouldn't be mad because the food is missing. She'd be mad that Angelica found out we eat crap. She'd be totally embarrassed for life. Oh, how did I get out of it?

I remind Chloe that if she tells, she will never ever get orange macaroni, red juice, or cookies again. Oh my gosh! She glared at me like she was burning a hole through my head, but the little brat shut right up.

Like I said, if you can find another way to make money, do it. But if you can't, and you jump into this abyss of no return, there are ways to passive-aggressively avenge yourself.

Instead of playing princess, I say, "I know, Chloe. Let's play a different game!" It's mean, I know it's mean, but I tell her I'm going to teach her "She Sells Sea Shells Down by the Sea Shore." I made her say it over and over, really fast, taped it on my phone, and will save it to blackmail her when she is older. Wanna see? It's messed up! I had to clean the spit off my phone.

I'm telling you, girl, if I knew then what I know now, I don't think I would do it. I mean I know you need the cash and all, but this babysitting stuff makes shoplifting look so tempting!

Convincing
Mrs. Coleman

Samantha Cardona

MAGGIE, 14

MAGGIE *is a high school girl who is never afraid to state her opinion. She talks a mile a minute when she is nervous, but will do whatever she can to get her point across. She is very uncomfortable with swimming during PE class and is trying every tactic possible to get out of it.*

MAGGIE   It's just that it's really demeaning. I'm not saying that PE isn't a good class to have, because it is. America has an obesity problem, we need to teach our kids to be healthier, the average teen watches forty hours a week of TV . . . blah, blah, blah—I get it. But must we include swimming? I mean look, there are plenty of exercises and activities that we can do as a class that don't require me to be half naked and wet in front of all the senior boys for sixty minutes every afternoon. Especially in front of Tanner Wallace who, let's face it, is the most beautiful creature at Jackson High. Maybe in the entire state of Illinois. And I'm not saying that I'm uncomfortable with my body. It's fine, I guess. It's just that I know I am not at my full pique of development. And it's really hard to feel confident with my tiny A-cups while Mandy Patterson is bouncing around in the pool with her balloon boobs right in front of Tanner. The women in my family develop late, okay?! And I don't think I should suffer because of that. I don't think anyone should. I'm sure that sophomore kid . . . what's his name? Pasty Pete? Yeah, I'm sure Pasty Pete is also not comfortable showing his body to everyone in class. It's hard being 6'1" and 125 pounds when you're a guy in high school. Especially when your skin reacts to the sun like that. Anyways, what I'm trying to say, Mrs. Coleman, is that I respect you. I respect your position as a female PE teacher, especially because I feel like it's a career that many women feel intimidated to break into. Yay feminism! Go you! But I'm really begging you to reconsider this swimming thing. I mean there are so many sports you haven't even considered yet. There's tennis, archery . . . I'm pretty sure ultimate Frisbee is starting to get a really big following.

[*Calmly, trying to be convincing.*]

Please, Mrs. Coleman, don't make me do this. I just don't want to put my kiwis on display until they've developed into grapefruits, you know what I mean? And if you can't do it for my kiwis, do it for everyone else. Think about the Pasty Petes of the world.

Sex Addicts Anonymous

Alessandra Rizzotti

JENNIE, 16

JENNIE *nervously stands at a podium at a Sex Addicts Anonymous meeting.*

JENNIE   Hello, my name is Jennie and I'm a sex addict.

[*After a deep breath.*]

Okay, I don't know if "addict" is the right word. I mean, I'm not looking to rename your whole organization, but I'm definitely sex "obsessed." I think about it all the time. Like . . . All. The. Time. Right now . . . and now. And yeah, definitely now.

I'm talking to you, but all I'm thinking about is Greg Johansen.

[*Thinking, then.*]

Wait, should I not say his name? Is he supposed to be anonymous? Shit. Sorry. It's just, I'm thinking about his abs. And his size 12 orange Nikes with the blue laces, his arm hair—which he shaves for swim meets—and his chin dimple. I don't think of it as a butt chin—it's a dimple. I don't care what Stephanie Marks says.

[*Thinking, then.*]

Yeah, I don't care if you know her name. She's a bitch. I said it. Stephanie Marks is a bitch.

This feels really good!

Anyway, Greg's chin dimple is cute. Super cute. I love it and I could probably just hole up and live right inside it.

But most of all, what I'm thinking about is . . . I'm thinking about having sex with Greg Johansen. Lots of sex. Lots of under the covers, no bra sex.

We haven't actually "done it" . . . yet. But we've come close. He said hi to me after Physics last week. Well, I think it was me. He waved down the hall and, yeah, it was to me.

Sure, I haven't actually "done it" with anyone. Yet. But when I do, it's definitely going to be Greg Johansen. Is licking a sex thing? I just want to lick him. I think about licking him a lot. I wonder what his elbows taste like. Kinda chlorine-y I'm sure. And salty and just yummy. See, I'm obsessed.

Wait, why is the moderator walking towards me? I should totally be here. I deserve to tell my story. I'm standing here, totally exposed.

[JENNIE *goes to leave and turns back.*]

Wait, it's like the Sex Addicts Anonymous law that you can't tell anyone about Greg, right?

Teen Angst

Carla Cackowski

JAX, 16

JAX, *dressed all in black, stands in front of a microphone. She does her best to be confident, but the pigtails that slip out from underneath her hoodie don't help the tough-girl image.*

JAX My name is Jax. Prepare to laugh, open-mic people. I mean, I can promise nothing, but you should be prepared just in case.

Sometimes my mother looks at me and says, "You're dressed like a serial killer." My response to that is always, [*Creepy voice.*] "Well Mom, I guess that means you're dressed like my next victim."

[JAX *is momentarily nervous. And then, as an aside:*]

Don't worry. I'm not really a serial killer.

[JAX *takes a deep breath and gets tough again.*]

My father was Son of Sam . . . My grandfather's name was Sam . . . My father never killed anything except for maybe my mother's spirit. My stepdad always says, "The problem with sixteen-year-olds is that they think they can joke about anything because they've experienced nothing." My stepdad is forty. The problem with forty-year-olds is that they are fat, balding fuck-tards.

[JAX *turns to someone in the front row and asks:*]

Where are you from?

[JAX *hears the answer.*]

I hate that place.

Sometimes my mom cries that she's afraid she gave birth to an unhappy child. I feel like it could be worse. She could've given birth to a vagina-chomping reptile. Last week my real dad sat me down at the dining room table and said that I like to say things just to shock people. Which is so not true . . . [*Quickly.*] I like to masturbate to *Dexter.*

[JAX *doesn't hear laughter. She pulls the hood of her sweatshirt down and gets real.*]

What the hell? This is some pretty funny stuff. I don't know what your problem is—you guys thought that fifty-year-old dude up here making jokes about his prostate was hilaaaaarious! I thought he was pretty boring. He didn't even ask for my phone number.

[*Beat.*]

Oh, I guess that red light means my time is up. Hey, Lighting Guy, I guess this finger means—

[*Just as she's about to flip her middle finger,* JAX *realizes—*]

Oh. Um . . . Can someone give me a ride home?

Dissection

Kate Mickere

JANE, 15 to 17

JANE *is in the guidance counselor's office.*

JANE Today was the day we were supposed to be dissecting fetal pigs in biology class . . . except my lab partner, Kevin Draper, fainted. One look at that curly little tail and one whiff of formaldehyde and he was on the floor.

Bridget, our other group member, had already been excused because she claimed that killing animals was against her religion. Puh-lease. Everyone knows she always takes an extra helping of meatballs on Spaghetti Wednesday. But all she had to do was bat her eyelashes and whine about the "inhumanity of it all" and Mr. Morrison let her sit in the next room and watch old *Bill Nye the Science Guy* tapes.

I've never tried to pull a stunt like that. The idea of me pretending to be Buddhist or something to get out of a pig dissection feels ridiculous. I'm really good at lying to my parents and friends . . . but with teachers? I don't have the guts. I've never even used my period as a way to get out of gym class.

Which is why I need you to let me drop Biology.

I am an artist. I'm meant to be an actor or a poet or someone that knows how to use a pottery wheel. All the schools I'm looking at are places where you can pick your own major. They won't care if I'm missing a year or two of science classes . . . or math classes, while we're at it. They just want me to be interesting.

[*Pause.*]

Okay. Yeah. It does seem a little weird that I'd want to drop a class that I had a decent B+ average in . . . but now Mr. Morrison is expecting me to dissect that pig all by myself! I mean . . . if I breathe through my mouth, I can probably manage to hack the thing up and get all of its body parts out. I'm not a weakling, like Kevin Draper. But he expects me to slice open that pig and write a lab report without any extension!

Everyone else is in groups of three or four. Why do I have to be punished because I can actually handle the sight of a dead animal? [*Beat.*] Maybe I was a butcher in a past life.

I just don't have time to get this thing done. Every day this week, I have tennis practice after school. After that, I have play practice on Monday, Wednesday, and Friday. Tuesday is spent at piano lessons and Thursday is for karate. I spend every study hall and lunch in the choir room, while Mr. Campbell shows me how to properly use my diaphragm. Yes, I am aware that that is a euphemism.

The weekends? Well, this weekend my mom is adopting a trio of Russian orphans and I have to help her choose the ones she likes best.

[*Beat.*]

Yes, that was a lie. I thought I'd try it since we discussed earlier how I'm not good at lying.

[*Pause.*]

Okay. So it's a no-go on the whole dropping Biology thing? All right. I just thought . . . I'd ask. I'll just take my pig and go.

[*She picks up a cardboard box, presumably holding her pig.*]

Yeah, that smell will linger for a while. Is it too early to talk about how I refuse to do Calculus next year?

Overachiever

Alessandra Rizzotti

ROBIN, 15

ROBIN *sits with a pile of books in front of her, studying for the SATs. She sips coffee and pops a caffeine pill. She's in the library, whispering to her study buddy, Barry.*

ROBIN   *Pssst*, Barry. Do you have any more caffeine pills? I have to stay awake during this five-part SAT practice test. I told my mom I'd come home with it all done after the library.

[*Barry hands her pills.*]

Oh man—thanks, Barry. Did you know they're making the essay section optional, by the way? When I was twelve years old, I was memorizing essays that I'd write for practice prompts and I'm so relieved that they don't do them anymore. Of course, I'll still do them for the real test, but it takes the pressure off, you know?

[ROBIN *tries to study, then gets distracted. She leans over to Barry.*]

Barry, can we take a break in like twenty minutes? I feel so fried and I just want to do some math games to take the edge off. Thanks.

[ROBIN *looks at her books, then looks back at Barry.*]

I can't wait till I'm at Harvard cruising along in class, without my mom breathing down my neck. She's such a drag. I feel like, ugh . . . dying around her. I'm not serious about that, but sometimes, oh man, I do feel like she makes me want to die of a caffeine pill overdose.

Sorry I keep bugging you. I need to do my relaxation exercises. I'm feeling like a mess.

[ROBIN *stares into space, not reading. She closes her eyes, and breathes in slowly, trying to meditate. She states affirmations.*]

It's going to be an awesome day. I can do this practice test. I can be a shining star.

[ROBIN *chants, whispering.*]

Sa. Ta. Na. Ma.

[ROBIN *turns to Barry.*]

I can't believe that we're going to be in SAT prep class for another three years. It just seems like, what's the point? Sometimes I wonder why I'm even going to college with the economic climate the way it is. You'd think they'd make up better ways to get degrees. Thank god there are those Codecademy places, you know? I should just be a software engineer and make apps for underprivileged youth to get better connected to resources, you know? Not sure how that works if they don't have phones, but that's all the rage these days, I hear. Diversity and tech. Tech for diversity.

Let's just quit, Barry! Let's quit school and be like Bill Gates! Then we can be billionaires and solve polio. Sigh. One day I'll be a philanthropist. One day I swear. So I can do yoga retreats way more frequently. Sorry to bug you. I know you're not doing well in the math sections, and I'm just distracting you again, I know.

[*Barry doesn't respond.* ROBIN *feels awkward.*]

I'm not messing with you, am I? Am I? Hey? Are you okay?

[*Barry doesn't respond.* ROBIN *realizes he's had headphones on the whole time.*]

O-M-G. Of course. You're wearing headphones. I'm an idiot.

[ROBIN *closes her eyes and breathes in.*]

You are aware. You are boundless. You are wonderful.

[*She chants.*]

Sa. Ta. Na. Ma.

Straight Guy

Joanna Castle Miller

STEPHANIE, 17

STEPHANIE *is in the school parking lot, a good while after the last bell.* STEPHANIE *has cornered Jeff, 16, near his car.*

STEPHANIE   No, no, Jeff. Don't apologize. Of course you're seeing someone. You're an athlete, you're . . . you're so hot. Handsome. She's lucky!

And it's a step up for me to flirt like this with a straight guy, even if you're taken or whatever. I mean, the only time a straight guy even asked me out was, like, middle school. I'm waiting for my mom and this sixth grader pulls out a fake rose, gets down on one knee, and says, "Fair Lady Stephanie, would you do me the great honor of escorting me to the ball?"

. . . Or something. It was so awkward. He looked like he was two. I told him all the usual things. You know—all the things you just told me. I wrote him off, and then I went to homecoming with Jeremy, who was really in love with Steve, which I found out from Steve . . . while he was breaking up with me.

All I've ever been is just a long beard to cover up two really confused guys.

A fat, oily beard.

And now it's prom and that's, like, the Big One. And I keep looking for that damn sixth grader to come back with his fake rose. But he's not coming back, Jeff. Let's face it, he was gay, too, and I'm not even beard material anymore. I have skin tags now, Jeff. Skin tags! I'm not even twenty and I already look like my mom! Eh, who am I telling? You've probably noticed already.

No? See? Here. Look.

I'll bet your girlfriend doesn't have skin tags. What was her name again? Jessie?

Oh, his name?

Oh, you're gay?

Oh, that's great. I mean it. I love gay guys.

I really love gay guys.

No Fear

Kate Ruppert

EMMA, 15

EMMA *is walking with a coffee, talking to a platonic, nerdy guy friend.*

EMMA   I mean, I guess I worry about a lot of things. Will there be a quiz . . . ? What if I get my period in the middle of class . . . ? Wait, is it a quiz or a test . . . ? I worry my zipper is down, or the button at my boobs is undone—all the time . . . Will I have enough money saved for camp . . . ? I worry the plane won't get off the ground during takeoff every time I fly . . . Will I make it to practice in time if I run home to get a snack first? Can I park here, or will someone ding the car and then I'll have to explain it to my dad . . . ? I'm so worried I'll accidentally spill coffee on my white jeans and I don't even have white jeans . . . Speaking of, do I look cute in these jeans, or will someone make fun of me . . . ? I'm always worried about my jeans. Do I look as good in a bathing suit as Maggie does . . . ? Do politics really affect me . . . ? Are these shorts too short for dress code . . . ? I'm worried I'll get in trouble . . . I'm worried someone will just start chasing me, and I'm scared of being chased, even in the middle of the day . . . Do my parents get me at all . . . ? I'm worried they never will . . . Exactly how early do I have to start thinking about college . . . ? What if I get pregnant . . . ? Sometimes, I worry about whether I'm adopted and my parents have been lying to me for fifteen years . . . Or am I really seventeen, you know . . . ? Can I wear

this color pink and not look too girly . . . ? I think I have to lose
five pounds . . . No, seriously, I don't think I'm ready for this test
and I have no idea what I want to be in life . . . Should I go with
Ali's family to France this summer . . . ? Or should I go with Kelly
and her family to the lake, because Mike will be at the lake . . . ?
I'm worried my sister will definitely tell my dad about the
cigarettes. Should I run for student council, honestly . . . ? I'm
nervous flamingoes can just tip over too easily. What if I don't
want to have kids . . . ? What if I completely wreck the car and
don't just ding it . . . ? Why won't they just buy me my own
car . . . ? Did my sister borrow my jeans . . . ? Did my mom
borrow my jeans . . . ?!?! What if my dad hates Mike . . . ? What
if I don't actually get into ANY college . . . ? I worry koalas can
easily fall out of their trees. And I worry about all those kids in
Africa. Why can't I look like her . . . ? What if I decide I don't
want to go to college at all . . . ? How come I never get asked
out . . . ? Is it the color pink I wore . . . ? Do you think he noticed
me . . . ? He probably just noticed the huge zit on my face . . . Is
this blue too boyish, or is it cute . . . ? Why won't my bangs do
what they're supposed to do . . . ?!?! Are my parents going to
embarrass me . . . ? How do I tell my mom I'm having sex . . . ?
No; my parents cannot know I'm having sex . . . How can I make
a difference . . . ? I have AP classes, I don't have TIME to make a
difference . . . All this, I worry about it all, all the time.

But do I worry that we're going to be invaded by aliens and will
they implant like a chip in my brain or something?! Um, no,
don't be ridiculous.

A Week in the Life of Phillip Jones

Bri LeRose

ALEAH YOUNG, 14

ALEAH YOUNG *is reading/giving a speech at the front of her English classroom.*

ALEAH   I know a boy named Phillip Jones, and I think you'll wish you knew him too. Phillip is bald—the only teenager I know who shaves his own head. He's got a gap in his teeth and he stands a foot taller than the rest of the kids in our grade, which actually serves him well. It makes up for his lisp, notorious gas issues, and general ridiculousness. The rest of the kids don't mess with Phillip, but they act like they hate him. I don't blame them, really—that kid has a gold medal in distracting everyone around him. But how could anyone hate someone who brings nothing but joy into the world? Let me paint you a picture of a week in the life of Phillip Jones.

On Monday, Phillip got a pass to the bathroom during English class. He raised his hand, signed Ms. Rodriguez's bathroom log, and agreed to be back in three minutes. Simple enough, right? Well, eight minutes later, Phillip returned to find our class working silently. He went up to the teacher and loudly explained, "Thorry Msth Rodriguesth. I had to get sthome toilet paper from Mr. Sthmith." She chuckled and told him "No problem, Phillip.

You can sit down," at which point Phillip's friends began to laugh their butts off and called him nasty. Ms. Rodriguez has a soft spot for Phillip and a very hard, gristly spot for bullies, so she pointedly reminded his friends that they all poop, too. Phillip stood up, wheeled his bald head around and yelled, "YEAH!" So that was Monday.

On Tuesday, Phillip got called up to the board in math class to solve a problem. He stood at the board dancing, tapping his foot to some beat in his head that didn't exist to the rest of us. He swayed back and forth, looking like Gumby—all arms and legs flopping about. Mr. Apman giggled. "Phillip, maybe less dancing, more solving." Phillip didn't miss a beat. "I gotta sthtop that or I'm gonna repeat thisth grade." Everybody paused, confused about why someone would be held back for dancing at the board. "Dude, what?" asked Corey, confused and maybe a little impressed. Phillip explained: "I'm alwaysth laughing and fooling around. My behavior isth not good." Mr. Apman, who also apparently has a soft spot for Phillip, tried to reassure him. "Phillip, you've been turning in homework lately—you're doing much better." He blushed, scribbled an answer on the board, and happily said, "No I'm not!" before running back to his seat and hiding behind his math folder. Mr. Apman checked his answer— no corrections needed. Well done, Phillip.

On Wednesday, we were packing up our stuff in homeroom. Everyone was running all over the place, yelling, jumping over chairs and throwing each others' backpacks around. I noticed Phillip staring out the window, quietly humming something to himself. I inched closer to hear a bit better. [ALEAH *sings the jingle*.] "It'sth a pillow, it'sth a pet. It'sth a pillow pet." I smiled and backed away. Later, on the bus, I asked Phillip why he was singing the jingle for Pillow Pets at the end of the day, and he flat-out denied doing it. At first, I thought he was embarrassed, but when I realized he's pretty much never been embarrassed in his life, it hit me: he just . . . he didn't know he was humming it out loud. I smiled and hummed it to myself. *"It's a pillow, it's a pet. It's a pillow pet."*

On Thursday, Ms. Martin had us practicing Cause and Effect in history class. She had us doing Yo Mama jokes, because she thinks she's hip, which she kind of is, because of that big, weird tattoo on her arm, but anyway. Everybody was a little uncertain—it's no fun to try to make a street activity school-appropriate, you know? Phillip had been silent the whole time, scribbling furiously in his notebook. Finally, just as everybody was running out of lame, safe jokes, Phillip raised his hand. He stood up, cleared his throat, and read off his page:

"Because yo mama's breath is so hot, as a result, she burned off my eyebrows when she breathed on me. Because yo mama is so stupid, as a result, she looked at her umbilical cord when giving birth and thought her baby came with cable. Because yo mama is so fat, as a result, she sat on the St. Louis Arch and it turned into a McDonald's sign." Then he sat back down and smiled.

On Friday, we were reading a short story by Dorothy Parker in English class. Ms. Rodriguez was reading the first part out loud, but she stopped when a bunch of kids sitting around Phillip started murmuring and laughing. She gave us her steely teacher stare and everybody froze. Morgan took over reading out loud as Ms. Rodriguez looked for the source of the distraction. She only made it a few minutes before kids started laughing again. "C'mon dude!" shouted Corey. I stretched my neck to see what was going on. Ms. Rodriguez raised her eyebrow, and Martez couldn't take it anymore. "Phillip's in here eating a pork chop!" he yelled. A pause. "Ms. Rodriguez, he's eating a pork chop and it's wrapped in a piece of loose-leaf paper." Ms. Rodriguez looked stunned, and Phillip sat there, not even attempting to deny it. Nobody knew yet whether or not it was okay to laugh, and the room was so silent that you'd be able to hear a single piece of pencil lead ring out as it hit the ground. But finally, Ms. Rodriguez let a sly little smile creep across her face and said, shaking her head, "Phillip, I can't believe I have to say this to you, but please stop eating a pork chop in the middle of first period." Corey chimed in: "Yeah dude, you couldn't wait 'til lunchtime?" Again, Phillip didn't miss a beat: "It woulda gotten cold by lunch." We laughed. All of us. And Morgan kept reading and Phillip kept eating. After all, he had a point.

I don't know much about Phillip Jones outside of school, or who his friends are, or if he has a girlfriend who goes to another school, or if his parents are nice to him. But I do know that I look forward to every class I have with him, and that a week in the life of Phillip Jones is a week I'm happy to be a part of. That's why I've chosen him as the subject of my "Most Inspiring Person" essay. Now if you don't mind, Phillip and I have gotta get to lunch. C'mon, Phillip.

[ALEAH *reaches into her pocket and pulls out something shaped like a porkchop wrapped up in a piece of loose-leaf paper, which can then be thrown at an audience member if desired.*]

Best Friends . . . for Never?

Andy Goldenberg

STACIE, 16

STACIE *breaks up with her friend in her friend's bedroom.*

STACIE   [*Inhales deeply.*] We have to break up.

I'm sorry, Stacey, but I can't keep hanging out on your couch and watching reruns and pretending to laugh and reminisce when I know that we're never going to make it in the long term. You were my first real best friend and we always said it would be forever and, lately, it's just kind of really been scaring me. I've never had another best friend. I don't know what that would be like. And I know that at some point in the future, I would resent you for labeling us as BFFs and not having the guts to stand up and make that kind of decision on my own. I went along with it back in second grade, but I've been unhappy for a while now, afraid to call it quits.

I stood by you when you were Team Edward. I thought it was cute when you swore yourself to Peeta. And you always loved Ron more than Harry. But, now, you're all into costume jewelry and heavy makeup and manis and pedis and we're just completely and utterly different. Your favorite color is hot pink. Mine is purple. You're blonde. I'm brunette. You like your coffee hot. I like mine cold. I mean, really, when you get down to it, the only thing that we have in common is the very thing that brought us together in the first place. Our name. But, even then, you spell "Stacey" with an *e-y* and I spell mine with an *i-e*. We're different!

I'll pinky swear you right now that there's nobody else. I pinky swear it. Yes, I've been seen out a lot with those valley girls, as I'm sure you know, but I promise I haven't been hanging out exclusively with any single one of them. I really like Beth, but I don't necessarily think she's bestie material. Maybe Winnie—she's funny and really knows how to throw a party. I swear it'll never be Staycee. Not just because she has your name, our name, but also, it's so weird to spell it with a y and two e's. Right? Plus, I really don't like the perfume she wears. To be totally honest, I'm kind of excited to just be known as an individual at the moment, you know?

[STACIE *reaches into her pocket.*]

Here's your necklace. I'd feel weird keeping one half of it when I can't uphold the very claim that it advertises. We're friends. And we'll always be friends, but best? Best friends? It's an adjective that I just don't think applies to us anymore. It's gold anyways, and, if we were really that close, you'd know that I only wear silver.

Cyndi for Goth Club President

Kayla Cagan

CYNDI, 15 to 17

CYNDI *is in the courtyard at her high school, where she and her friends eat lunch every day.* CYNDI *addresses her fellow sophomore goth friends—Billy, Sarah X, Crimson, and Alex—during lunch.*

CYNDI Hey, You Guys. It's really great that you stayed during lunch to be a part of this deeply important electoral process. I won't freak out or anything, but I think you know how excited I am. I'm this excited.

[CYNDI *pauses and stares at the club in front of her.*]

I know you think Alex is a worthy-ish candidate, but like, I have one question for you. Is Alex McCain really the Right Knight of Darkness for this year's gathering of the Goths? Uh, no. Not even close.

How could he know what you want? He hasn't sat up nights with all of you, listening to your daily tragedies, weeping with you over each and every breakup, painting your nails every shade of heartache: Black, Jet Black, Ebony Black, Black Black, Black Black Black, Blah Black, Bah Bah Black Sheep Black, 50 Shades of Black, Black Is Back, and of course, Best Black Ever. I've been with you through every hair color, every liquid eyeliner, and every piercing—except for that one, Billy. I still feel bad about that, but you know I couldn't get out of detention that day. I was with you in deep, despairing spirit, though.

[CYNDI *makes a heartfelt gesture.*]

So why should I, Cyndi La Force, be your new Goth Club president? Because I care. I care with every beautifully sad bone in my body, with every red blood cell that carries the iron in my hemoglobin. I care. When you're sad, I'm sad. When you're happy, I'm sad that I'm not as happy as you are but also happy that you are happier than me, even if this world doesn't have much meaning in the long run and happiness is just a social construct created by people like my parents who bankrupt their vapid emotions in desperate commercials and buying shiny new cars.

I believe it was John Paul Sartre who said, "Everything has been figured out, except how to live." And I agree with that, and I know you do, too. Everything is preordained. It's all there. Whether I want to be pale or not, I am pale . . . because that's just how it is and how it will always be. Also, I don't like to go outside, so that helps.

But Alex certainly hasn't figured out how to live the life of a true goth, one that not only expects the darkness of the world around him, but invites it over and gives it a flat soda of sadness. Alex keeps hoping things will get better, that he can make a difference for us. But that's not my president.

My ideal president lets us be who we are, mumble what we want, and enjoy all of the cloudy days of high school within us, besides us—not hanging out in the pizza line in the cafeteria. I'm not against pizza, but I'm against lines. Nothing about us is straight. We're circular, like the life—or should I say "death"—cycle.

Billy, Sarah X, Crimson, and even you, Alex—you all know who I am. I'm Cyndi "Siouxsie" Johnson and I'm not just your friend, I'm the very picture of you. I'm you, I'm you, [*Dramatic pause.*] and I'm you. I'm your next Goth Club President, and I promise, if elected, that I will make you very happy, which is to say, keep you very sad, in all the empty, beautiful ways that matter. I thank you for your time, but more than that, I thank you for your lives, which are limited, but very real . . . for now.

The floor is now open to questions.

Admissions

Leah Mann

LAYLA B., 17

High school senior LAYLA B. sits eagerly across the desk from a college admissions officer. She slides her art portfolio closer to his face.

LAYLA   Did I show you my new painting? It's really good, not to brag or anything, but I'm proud of it.

[*Beat.*]

So yeah, that's me. Well, based on me. It's sort of a self-portrait but with artistic liberties, and that's an octopus entwined around me. I'm fascinated by sea creatures and sexuality—it's an interest of mine, you know, like the intersection of the two? Honestly, I've been pretty repressed sexually, for most of my life, and am just starting to explore that side of myself.

[*Beat.*]

Sure, I'm only seventeen. You COULD say that I haven't been sexually repressed so much as just, like, a kid or in high school, but there are plenty of kids in my school who have been sexual for a while now and I was always too scared. I got my period when I was twelve, but this year was the first time I even really made out with anyone.

[*Beat.*]

Which I have totally done now, a bunch of times, because I'm not weirded out anymore. I'm an artist so I have to express myself, and using my body and sensuality is just one more way to do that. It's another language, like learning Spanish only the human body is universal so it's like Esperanto but that everyone actually knows. It's not just about sex, okay, I'm not like a nympho or anything. I haven't even HAD sex. It's about trust and vulnerability.

[*Beat.*]

Sea creatures? Oh, I don't want to explain too much, because art is open to interpretation and has different meanings for everyone.

[*Beat.*]

To me? It represents how alien another person can be, but that you can still be intimate with someone on a super deep level without knowing them superficially. Plus I love the ocean and the shapes of sea creatures, and the juxtaposition of something that's supposed to be cold and slimy with a warm, hot-blooded woman is very symbolic.

[*Beat.*]

I'm very into symbolism.

[*Beat.*]

For example, you are wearing a tie and holding a nice leather notebook. That symbolizes your status and seriousness and that in our relationship, you have the power. Which is honestly, kinda ridiculous because I have lots of colleges that I could go to. I mean, you should want me as a student as much as I want to go here. It's about a good match for both parties, right? I want things from the school, but the school wants things from its students—and not just the tuition money.

[*Beat.*]

Not that I don't respect the system, but the system should be questioned, obviously. That's what you should want in a student—someone who's inquisitive and doesn't take things at face value. That's me. I am so not interested in the status quo. I'm not just an artist, I'm a thinker and a leader.

[*Beat.*]

I'm most looking forward to finding myself as a person. I've started the journey already, which is what I've been showing you in my art. I know that when I'm away from home, surrounded by other kids who are smart like I am, that I'll grow even more.

[*Beat.*]

Like here's a painting I did three months ago of a mermaid stranded in the desert, which is technically accomplished but lacking nuance. It symbolizes how lost you can be in the world— like at my school I never really fit in . . . I mean I was popular, but always different—like this beautiful mermaid dying in a barren desert. And only like two months later, I did this portrait of an old woman holding a dead squid—here, the imagery symbolizes, like, life and death and growing apart from your family. See what I mean? I got so much better in just two months—imagine what I'll be doing in a year!

[*Beat.*]

My top choice? I believe in always sharing my true self, so honestly—I want to defer for at least a year and go explore the world and other cultures. I worked super hard in high school, like crazy hard and got perfect grades, which is probably why I was never dating or doing fun stuff, and now I'm sick of homework and papers and reading.

[*Beat.*]

Which is why I feel like this school would be a good match. I mean, it's hard and has a good reputation, but it's not THAT hard. Not to be rude or anything, but you know, I mean, you went here.

[*Beat.*]

That's it?

[*Beat.*]

It was interesting meeting you, too. You're getting up from your desk; that symbolizes an ending, but every ending is also a beginning. I'm very Zen about these things, because I'm an old soul.

[*Beat.*]

Wow, good handshake. You totally speak the universal language of touch. Very firm and decisive. I just learned a lot about you.

Unhooked

Keisha Cosand

ASHLEY, 16

ASHLEY *is talking to a boy named Andy, who she agreed to hook up with. The monologue is set in* ASHLEY's *living room, after school, before her parents get home from work.* ASHLEY *and Andy are 16.*

ASHLEY Um . . . Yeah . . . I don't want to do this. I know your pants are down. Yeah, I can see that. I changed my mind. I think I just had an epiphany. "A-pif-anee!" It means "big idea," "lightbulb moment," an "a-ha"! Because of what's in your pants? No. Well, maybe. That's not what I mean, though.

Seriously. This is stupid. I see you at school, and sometimes you say hi and sometimes you don't. You made it clear that I'm cool, we are just friends, and it is better to keep things uncomplicated. You want to know what's uncomplicated, Andy? A vibrator is uncomplicated—it's quick, less messy, and works every time.

I'm buttoning my shirt because I want things to be complicated. I want to have a crush, I want to fall in love, I want to stay up and talk all night on the phone. I want to take things slow and mean it. I want to be wanted for real, for more than one hour. I'm sick of hooking up. Who even decided this was a good idea? Did you and some of your buddies get in a room and write some kind of creed? "Let us be selfish and make them chase us; let us force them to watch sports and insist they pretend to like it; we shall speak few words and make them do our homework; we won't stay with them very long, and we will convince them that hookups are cool, and they like them too; let us make them believe less is more, and this is love!" Screw that! How could we be so stupid? No, I don't think you are stupid. Well, you do kinda suck at math. I mean girls. All this time, I've been pretending you like me, or that you will change and really like me. That's why I came here. Now you know.

Yes, Andy, I'm going to tell all my friends. I'm going to tell them we didn't "do it." That we never did it. True, they will probably tell your friends. Of course I'm sorry if it ruins your reputation.

You want to cuddle? Now? I don't believe you. No, I don't think you're being sincere. Oh, now you want to talk. Let me guess, you're going to take me to dinner and a movie. Come on. Zip it up. I'll take you home. Not to my house, Andy, to your house. Are you kidding? I'm not going to walk you to your door. No, get up, let's go! This wasn't a mistake; it was almost a mistake. Okay, I'll hold your hand. Just please don't cry. Jeez!

Dude! I said zip it up!

Our Parents

Rachel Paulson

MEGAN, 16

MEGAN *and her little sister Katy, 14, are grounded in their bedroom for throwing a party while both parents were out of town.* MEGAN *now recounts to Katy all the times that she has been in trouble with their parents and warns Katy of what's to come when Katy reaches high school.*

MEGAN   Our parents are so annoying. I mean, how did they find out? We covered up everything perfectly! Maybe we didn't get the Pin the Tail on the Freshman poster from the garage? Seriously, what is wrong with them? It's ONE party.

It's not enough that they pick you up every day from school—just wait until you get into high school—that becomes the worst thing. In the world. They won't let you take the bus till sophomore year for sure. Wait until you meet a cute boy. One time, Mom showed up to pick me up from a party. In a Volvo! I mean how embarrassing is that? I had finally made it to something Matt Morrison had invited me to, it was Senior Skip Day, and he invited me to go to a house and hang out with him and his friends while they play video games. So cool right? I know. Anyway, I lied to them (and you and I both know they always know when we are lying). I told them I was going to be in school—of course! I couldn't tell them I was going to skip school for the hottest, most popular guy in the world. Anyway, I went to the guy's house, and they were smoking pot. I didn't smoke, I've never been around anyone who has, I guess I'm a good kid or something. A nerd. Mom called my school to ask them some question about a PTA meeting—I know what you're thinking, Mom is on the PTA? So embarrassing, right? They told her I wasn't in school today, and she texted me fifty times! FIFTY TIMES. I hadn't gotten those many text messages since my best friend broke up with her girlfriend (I have SO many gay friends). I realized I was in trouble and panicked. I had to lie, since I couldn't tell Matt and his friends that Mom was mad at me, I mean what a loser. I told Matt that you were in a car wreck—I know that's bad, but what was I suppose to do—it also covered for the fact that she told me she was going to come and pick me up. I quickly grabbed my backpack and told Matt I was going to wait outside for Mom. When she pulled up—she was screaming at the top of her lungs, "Mary! You're in big trouble young lady!" Then, I looked behind me and realized Matt and all of his friends were standing behind me listening and laughing. I bowed my head and got into the front seat. Matt still asks me about how "my younger sister" is doing. He never invited me anywhere ever again.

So, Katy, you better get some good lies ready for next year, 'cause Mom knows everything. You're going to need them.

Girls Like Us

Jennifer Dickinson

IZZY, 14

IZZY is in a church. Lights come up on a podium. Next to the podium is an open casket. IZZY, uncomfortable in her stuffy clothes, stands behind the podium.

IZZY   I wasn't going to speak today, but I'm so sick of hearing how ladylike Aunt Carla was. Aunt Carla wasn't ladylike. She was fierce. She's the reason I know how to play baseball. She told me once, I have the strongest arm of any girl she's seen pitch. After I threw my last no-hitter, my mom took me to Shake Shack for a cherry cone to celebrate. Aunt Carla used to love that place. Unfortunately, my sister went, too. [IZZY *looks for her sister, Janine, in crowd, then waves.*] Hi, Janine. It really sucks when your sister calls you a pig for the way you eat. [*Back to the rest of the group:*] Janine and Mom are obsessed with their weight.

Morning at my house goes like this. Mom and Janine high-five after sprinkling one-fourth a teaspoon of brown sugar on their grapefruits—the only sugar they're allowed for the day. Then Janine packs lunch: six carrots and a tablespoon of crunchy almond butter. Mom swears she only eats apples while we're at school, but Janine found a Ziploc of Oreos inside the Bible and now she wants to install security cameras at home.

Mom, you should know Aunt Carla thought it was ridiculous that you had pictures of Heidi Klum plastered across our refrigerator door. She never believed you were searching for God. She said your God is Heidi Klum.

Last night, when Janine took down those pictures, I thought things were going to change. But then Janine said Mom should have a new thinspiration, and handed her a picture. Of Mom. On her wedding day. Some of you were there but I've never seen her in a dress before and her smile seemed real, the way she looks when she eats one-fourth of a devil's food cupcake. She's so tiny you can see her chest bone poking out, and Janine pointed to Mom's bone and said: "Banish weakness."

Mom started crying and told Janine to burn the photo. But Janine stuck it in Heidi Klum's old place, right next to my baseball schedule. I said maybe Mom and Janine should break a sweat once in a while. Maybe if their bodies felt stronger, they wouldn't be so weak around food. I thought that was pretty genius, but Janine rolled her eyes and told me I don't understand bodies and I should go on a diet, too.

But I do understand bodies. So did Aunt Carla. Did you know her favorite painter was Degas? She said the Degas women were like her. Their bodies have wrinkles and lumps. They look healthy.

I was there the day she found out she was sick. You should know she didn't cry. Or freak out. Or anything you'd expect. She made me go outside with her, in the rain, and swim in the river. She raced me to the first rock and she won. She told me she would beat the cancer.

Mom made me look in the casket. For closure, she said. But I don't feel closed. I feel like I've been busted wide open. Aunt Carla doesn't look like the Degas paintings anymore. Her cheeks are gray and hollowed out and someone smeared red lipstick across her mouth. She looks so scary. I tried to wipe the lipstick off, but Janine pulled me away. She said I was being disrespectful. But Aunt Carla hated makeup. She looked beautiful exactly the way she was. She told me I did, too.

The girls at school call me fat and ugly. It's a fight not to believe them. But If Aunt Carla were here, I know she'd tell me to keep fighting. She'd promise me I can win.

Bambi-Sue's Unfortunate Nickname

Kate Ryan

BAMBI-SUE, 17

As BAMBI-SUE *gets ready for the dance, she explains to her prom date (her Uncle Billy) how she got her nickname. Her boobs spilling out of a too-tight tube dress, she rolls empty beer cans in her hair, using them as curlers.*

BAMBI-SUE   Okay, you know what, Uncle Billy, let me just tell you how I got this nickname so yer not confused, alright? It's not a real funny story, alright? It's a pretty freakin' boring story if ya ask me. When you hear people tell stories about how they got cool nicknames—nicknames like Motown Maverick or Billy the Tank or Ham Sandwich McGillicutty—it usually has somethin' to do with that time they wrestled a gator out of the hot tub or lassoed a pig with nothin' but a toothbrush and a hair tie. But not me. Nope. There are three other Bambi-Sue Jacksons at my high school when there ain't even a thousand people here in Jeffersonville! 'Cause that's just my luck, I guess.

[BAMBI-SUE *sighs and grabs another beer can, wrapping her hair around it.*]

What's even better is they took up all the good versions of my family name. There's Bam Bam, Bambi J—she sometimes goes by Bambarella—and Sue Jack. Sue Jack! Isn't that kickass? And to put salt in the wound, they're the nicest, finest ladies you'll find in all of Georgia, too.

[*She stuffs a handful of chips in her mouth and applies a thick layer of hot pink lipstick while she chews.*]

Listen, I know what yer thinkin'. Yer thinkin', Bambi, why didn't you just come up with an equally awesome name for yerself, girl? It's not that hard! Well, let me tell you, honey, I tried. Boy, did I try! I tried to make Bumble Bee work, Bambilyn Suzanne, Black Belt Bambi (seein' how I love taekwondo and all)—even Evelyn! But not a single frickin' one stuck, gosh dern it.

[*She takes a bite out of a Twizzler, then proceeds to wrap a strand of hair around it.*]

It just so happens that one day, while I was lamentin' all this nickname nonsense, I comforted myself sick with a big ol' bowl a three-bean Frito chili. Well, don't you know it, I had the worst gas of my lil ol' life. And just because of my stinkin', no good luck, we were doin' jumpin' jacks in PE that day when I just couldn't hold it in any longer. So you know what I did? I let 'er rip. And let me tell you—that fart made its way ten miles to town and back. Geeeeezus it stank! And from that moment on, I knew there was no goin' back, no changin', no skippin' town without my new, God-given nickname, Turd Ferguson. That's right, capital T-U-R-D Ferguson. Man! That's just my luck, ain't it?

[*She jams her feet in six-inch stilettos and sprays perfume all over her body.*]

But thanks for takin' me to prom, Uncle Billy. When we ride up in your kickass Ford Pinto we'll show all them kids how pretty I really am. Make 'em think twice before they call me a turd again. Now let's go before they run out of pizza bagels!

The Bat Mitzvah Speech

Jessica Glassberg

SUZANNA COHEN, 13

SUZANNA COHEN, *timidly nerdy and sweet, stands on the pulpit, nervously addressing her family, friends, and congregation at her bat mitzvah.*

SUZANNA Thank you so much, Rabbi Cohen, for that incredible introduction.

[SUZANNA *is totally sincere.*]

But I don't *actually* study twenty-four hours a day. I sleep. And I eat. And I like to watch *Matlock* reruns. So, yeah, in the case of Suzanna Cohen versus studying all day, the defense rests.

[*She nervously laughs at her lame Matlock/lawyer joke.*]

So, this week's *parsha* is about bravery. And Rabbi, you called me brave for becoming a bat mitzvah. And, my parents told me I was brave for being me, and my school counselor says I'm brave like every week. Even my gynecologist, who I now see because I truly have become a woman and menstruate, she says I'm brave for going to her. And most of you might think I'm brave because you know I'm pretty shy.

Sure, you could say it's brave to stand up here in front everyone in the entire seventh grade. Well, everyone who didn't go to

Rachel Klein's cruise ship bat mitzvah, which was also today. So, like the ten of you who didn't get your RSVP in in time for Rachel Klein's cruise ship bat mitzvah. But I'm happy to have you "all aboard" the S.S. Suzanna.

[SUZANNA *exaggeratedly points to herself.*]

SUZANNA.

[*Awkwardly clarifies.*]

But my bat mitzvah theme isn't a cruise. It's reading. You'll all be going home with the complete works of Nabokov. In Russian! *Ypa!* [*Translation: "Cheers!"*]

[SUZANNA *starts getting anxious.*]

Anyway, I know I'm brave just because I'm here. Ya see, I have been having nightmares about opening the Torah ark.

[*She gets more anxious.*]

Not just because this is a big day, and when you open the Torah ark it's a beautiful moment in becoming a woman.

[*Even more anxious.*]

But, I picture those ghost things flying right out like at the end of *Raiders of the Lost Ark*, and that my face completely melts off like the Nazi dudes.

[*Hyperventilating.*]

Sometimes, I'm the guy with the fire coming out of my eyes, and I burn all of you to bits and then my face explodes. But usually my face melts off.

[*Huge exhale.*]

So, *mazel tov* to all of us for our faces not melting off . . . yet!

I have to go throw up now, but please join me and my family for a hosted *kiddush* in the youth lounge. We've got lox!

Middle-School Preparedness Tips

Rachel Pollon

LINDSAY BUTLER, 14 to 15

LINDSAY *sits in a reclining chair in the Butler family living room across from the three girls who sit side by side on the family couch.*

LINDSAY   The reason I've gathered you here today is in an effort to offer you some tools you'll need to best navigate the inevitable pitfalls of seventh grade. Being well ensconced in the ninth grade, I have the advantage of having recently enough lived the journey you'll soon be embarking on that the memories are still incredibly potent. And as your sister, your best friend's sister, and the sister of the girl you've volunteered to tutor I feel it is my duty to impart this information while the wisdom I've gained these last illuminating years will be of the utmost value to you. I only wish I'd had someone do this for me.

It started out like any other day: your basic Southern California fall morning. I was a typical thirteen-year-old girl, midway through the first semester of seventh grade. I rode the fine line between feeling pretty confident I knew everything and being entirely insecure with no idea where I fit in.

It seemed there had to be an answer, a golden ticket, a holy grail that—if I could just get my hands on it—would make me feel complete, never question my status in school, never worry about whether guys thought I was pretty, and for a bonus, let me magically know what "frenching" was because I was too embarrassed to ask.

So, it was like any other day. The school bell rang at eight a.m., I hadn't studied hard enough for my History quiz, Jordan Klein still didn't seem to notice me—status quo. The only thing that set this day apart, the one detour on the road of my pretty par-for-the-course life was the utter excitement I was filled with . . . about the fact that for my first time ever . . . I was wearing my new high-heeled Korky's to school. In case you are unfamiliar, Korky's are a high-heeled sandal, made of light beige leather, with a wedged base made of cork.

There are two types.

One is a milder version, with a gradual raise in height from ground level at the toe to two inches at the heel.

The second version is the more grown-up pair. Platforms. Cork wedge starting at about two inches in front and gradually getting higher through the heel. You're basically walking on a soft brick.

I'd had the milder pair since sixth grade—I should add that this milder pair had rainbow stripes on the cork, making what they lacked in danger at least a little more festive—and was graduating to the more evolved, high-heeled pair. I aspired to them. I wanted to be what they represented: foxy, mature, sure of myself. Everything that I wasn't was guaranteed in the crannies of those corked heels. I wanted in. I wanted to crawl into those crannies and emerge awesome.

My Korky's and I made it through first period (Homeroom) and second period (Spanish) with relative aplomb. Missy Kaufman's eyes went wide and she gave me a thumbs-up from across the room after watching me walk up to the front of the class to write the first-person present tense of "to look" in Spanish on the chalkboard. (It's "busco," if you're interested.) But other than that, most people didn't seem to notice. This was slightly disappointing, but I tried to chalk it up to a heretofore unknown-to-me general consensus that I was cool enough to wear the shoes and that it wasn't anything to make a big deal about.

When Nutrition Break came after second period, I went about my morning as per usual, heading over to the grassy area in the middle of campus to share a snack with my two best friends, Stephanie and Christy. It was Christy's day to bring the snack, and I was looking forward to it because I didn't have time to eat breakfast after going back and forth deciding which jeans to wear my with new shoes. Flares were daring, overalls said it was no big deal. I went all in with the flares.

As I rounded the corner of the last building before stepping on to the grass, I heard someone call my name. I didn't recognize the voice, but turned, and as I did stepped onto a liquid mass on the walkway just behind me. Things started to feel like they were going in slow motion. I felt the squooshiness, the slickness. I felt my right foot wobbling from side to side as the cork brick below it started to buckle. I felt myself drop the lip gloss I was about to apply, on the off chance Jordan decided to talk to me on the lawn, and then slowly sink as my left foot took allegiance with my right and wobbled itself over and onto the ground.

Everything went quiet. No one was immediately by my side. I had instinctively covered my eyes with my right arm as I laid splayed out on the walkway, my head miraculously pillowed by my backpack that I fell on like a perfect cushion. Finally after

what seemed like hours but was most likely only seconds, I heard
chatter and people gathering.

I felt hands on my one dangling arm and various other hands on
my legs.
I heard someone ask, "Is she dead?"
I heard someone else say, "Oh my god, did she just trip in her
Korky's?"

Though my body was incapacitated momentarily, my mind was
not. My brain, in an effort of complete and utter self-
preservation, took a trip around the possibilities track and came
up with the answer.

I laid there for another long minute or so, and when I heard
someone say they would go get the nurse, I slowly let my limbs
twitch and raised my right arm away from my eyes and asked, in a
spot-on tone of a confused person, "Where am I?"

I was told I was at school. At Portola Junior High in Tarzana,
California.

I was told I fell.
"Oh my god," I said. "I must have fainted."

"Fainted?" a chorus of onlookers chimed back at me.

"Yes," I said more emphatically as I slowly rose to a seated
position, removing the straps of my backpack as I did so as not to
be dragged back down. "Because of my period. I'm having my
period today and I must have fainted."

I wasn't having my period. I hadn't even gotten my period yet.
But I knew some older girls who had and they always made a big
deal about it, and I thought I'd try my hand at it.

From then on I was the exotic girl with the high heeled Korky's who got her period earlier than most and therefore must be much more mature and interesting than anyone had previously given me credit for.

And so in summation, if it wasn't incredibly clear, seventh grade means being prepared to think on your feet even when you aren't actually standing on them, and aspiring to great heights even if there's a chance you might slip along the way. I hope one day you'll have the opportunity to pass this on to a little sister, a friend of a little sister, or as extra credit to a girl you meet who might need a little life tutoring.

Okay, let's bring it in. [*Puts her fist out for a group fist pump.*] "Girl power!"

Know-It-All

Brandon Econ

CLAIRE, 17

CLAIRE *is talking to her boyfriend, Marcus, outside a Dipp'n Dots.*
CLAIRE *met Marcus while buying a sitar at a Guitar Center during a*
phase of personal and emotional reinvention. She's immensely talented
but prone to distraction. While not naturally vacuous or superficial,
lately she's been having a "rough time."

CLAIRE   Marcus, I hate to say it, and I hope you don't get mad,
but, you're just not doing it for me right now.

Now, I know what you're going to say before you even say it,
"Claire, what the eff are you talking about?!" And that's the
problem. I already know what you're going to say. You're so
predictable. You have been since we started dating. I knew you
were going to ask me out, I knew you were nervous, and I knew
you'd try and play it off like it wasn't a date.

I knew effing everything.

I still do. Do you know how terrible of a burden that is? I have to
force all of the excitement. Or feign it at least when you show
some initiative. But I already know what ideas you're having and
how you're going to execute them.

Like already effing know.

You want to roll your eyes and say that I have it all wrong. That's just like you. You always do that! You don't effing change.

You're sweet and very kind but that only gets you so far. And don't get me wrong, I love how sweet you are and how kind you are, but I already know you're going to be sweet and kind and I just wish there was something more.

Listen, my father is pretty much my mom's little effing puppy . . . he does whatever she wants. He used to drink Guinness, he used to have a leather jacket, he used to drive a Corolla, but now he does none of that. He drinks sauvignon blanc, wears sweatpants, and drives a Ford Explorer. And yeah, that last one seems like an upgrade, but it's to serve a point. He filled a role and he lost his . . . you know, identity. His effing identity was a badass Navy pilot. Now he just does whatever my mom wants. I don't want that. I don't want you like that. But just in the past few months I get the impression that you'll do anything I effing want whenever I want it, and that's not what I want! That's not what I effing want. And I knew it was happening. And I don't effing want it to happen because I know it's going to and I don't want that because I don't want to know what's going to happen but that's what's happening and I effing hate it!

Don't say, calm down! I know that's what you want to say. I know it! I know you! You don't even know me. You don't. You've accepted the fact that I am who I am and you don't want to change that, and I don't want that Marcus. You know I don't want that, I know I don't want that so don't make it seem like you don't know that I knew that you wanted that because I do . . . I do know, okay!? OKAY!?!

Do you even have any wants, Marcus? I know you do. You want to be in a band, and you want to make music, and you don't want celebrity because that's a construct advertisers used to chain an individual's soul to their art so you're no longer making art to express but instead you're making art that's easily digestible for the huddled masses. I know that about you. You've been very clear. You saw that documentary on the band called "Death" and you've really latched on to that worldview. I get it. And I think that's awesome. I really dig that and it turns me on. I would like to kiss you but I can't because that's what I know you want me to do so I'll shut up but I won't because I know that already and I'm tired of knowing everything!!! I know everything and my head's going to explode, Marcus. Just effing explode from too much knowing.

I am all-seeing, all-knowing, and I'm tired of it! I am the eye of providence, and you are Charon, the ferryman of the damned!

[*Beat.*]

What?

[*Beat.*]

You wanted to break up, too? Why?

[*Beat.*]

I didn't know that.

Kicked Out

Alessandra Rizzotti

STACY, 17

STACY *is an unruly teen. She's had a traumatic upbringing and she's good when she's not emotional. Here, she slams the door open to a homeless shelter, and is speaking really loudly, in a state of unrest, to an intake coordinator there.*

STACY   It's me again! The cracked-out lady's daughter! The bitch kicked me out of the house again last night. She didn't want me in the living room because she had her convict boyfriend come over, and since the bedroom is in the living room because it's really a studio—well, you know how that went. Her vag seems to be more important than who came out of it!

[STACY *spreads her legs and laughs. She has a moment where drugs seem to kick in.*]

Don't look at my special parts! What's that you say, little man in the lady's computer??? Bee bop beep bop boop. You still got dial-up in here? What is he saying? I don't understand electricity! Speak louder, roboto man!

[STACY *disassociates from the computer and seems to become lucid again. She talks to the intake coordinator directly.*]

Does your friend in the computer have a room available? I just want to get some sleep. My legs and arms have been itching for hours and I was up till five a.m. under the freeway with some lady who Sharpied a drawing of an entire living room on the wall. She should design for IKEA. It was a paint-by-numbers, draw-your-own-home type of deal.

[*She sniffs her fingers.*]

I can trade labor for a room. Woah.

[*She stumbles and seems dizzy.*]

I gotta sit down. I had to take some of my mom's shit just so I could handle last night.

What?! Don't tell me that! Rodrigo told me I could come any time, clean or sober! He was my case manager. Call him. He will tell you. So what am I supposed to do? Stay outside? That could take weeks, and I don't have a tent. That would be intense. Get it?

[STACY *speaks quickly, as if the computer helped her come up with a solution.*]

I can work the kitchen again. Do you have that slot open? I'll do dishes if you give me gloves this time. I got a rash last time because I think I'm allergic to the nonorganic soap you guys use. So please, go all natural—it's all the same, by the way. Marketers think they're clever, but they're not.

[STACY *hits her ear repeatedly, which brings her into a lucid state.*]

I've been getting kicked out of the house every week so my mom could sell her body, but I don't want to move in with my girlfriend because her heart is made of holes and I'm a zombie around her. I told her, I'm like She-Hulk—stronger when enraged, muscly, and green. Basically, I can handle shit on my own. I should probably go to her house tonight, though, if you won't put me up . . .

[STACY *whips her head around.*]

Did you hear that? The aliens are coming! Dammit if you don't put me up, I'll be taken to Mars! Please! I have potential. I can show you proof of my B minuses from middle school and I worked at a KFC one time, making all the chicken finger-lickin' good, so I have a reference. Here, give me one night. I'll clean all the rooms in just a few hours like a Roomba on speed.

[STACY *stares at a wall for a few minutes. She daydreams. Her mind wanders. She hits her ear multiple times. She quickly snaps out of it and starts to cry.*]

Last time I almost killed myself and Rodrigo came to get me but he didn't answer this time and now he's not answering, and so everyone is leaving me. The aliens are all like, "E.T., come home," and I'm like, "I'm not E.T.! I'm not!"

[*She has a panic attack.*]

[*She breathes heavily.*]

I can't stay here on Earth because no one's letting me anymore. I'm too special for this planet! Oh god, my chest. That's not heartburn. It's heartbreak. I'll get through this, with or without myself! With or without you. With or without my girlfriend.

[*She puts her arms up, ready to be lifted up into the sky. Nothing happens. She stretches up again.*]

Are you there, God? It's me, not Margaret, your favorite, but Lamesha. Will you please give me a sign?

[*She looks at the person behind the desk.*]

Hey! You! Do you talk ever? You seem mute. Well, God is saying you're somehow my sign. You sure you don't have a room? My mind is in another galaxy right now and I need help.

Big Hero

Dana Weddle

CLAIRE, 14 to 16

CLAIRE *is in her living room; it is 2:00 a.m. The scene is performed in one big rant.*

CLAIRE   Mom. Listen to me. No, we don't need to "have the talk." No, Mom. Stop YELLING. Mom! You didn't wait too long. I'm fourteen, Mom—I already know all that stuff. I mean, not like THAT. No, Mom! They told us all that stuff at school. Like, a LONG time ago. Whatever, it doesn't even matter. It's not what you think! Listen! Mom. Sit down. Will you just sit down and listen to me? Or keep standing. Sure. Keep standing. Just listen. Please. Okay? Are you listening? Okay—Are you crying? Geez, Mom. You're seriously overreacting to this.

Now, I didn't lie to you . . . well . . . not really. I only half-truthed. Mom! You are supposed to be listening! You are totally freaking out for no reason. No, I did NOT sneak out. You keep saying that, and it is definitely NOT what I did. What I *did* was go to spend the night at Sarah's, just like I told you I was going to. I was supposed to be at Sarah's house, sleeping in the nighttime. The time that is night and is reserved for sleeping was when I was going to be there. I did not *lie* about that. And yes, at some point in time while I was at Sarah's, in the earlier part of the evening that is not the sleeping time, I did *leave*—I did what you would call "leave" her house. I did *leave* her house for what I *thought* would be a brief period of time. I went to the store to get some snacks for movie night. Since it was Friday the 13th, we were gonna watch some old slasher—I MEAN—Disney movies. Age-appropriate Disney movies . . . are . . . what . . . we were watching . . . ahem . . . *ANYway*, so I went to the grocery store and it just so happened that Jamie was working. Well, about to be done working, but he was there, at the store when I got there. You know Jamie. [CLAIRE *smiles.*] He's so tall. His hair is so curly and unruly—like, crazy thick curls—and he wears those cute nerd glasses, but in an ironic way . . . [*Daydreaming, drifting off.*] The coolest, most ironic kind of way . . . He's really smart. He plays bass for The Fuzzy Handcuffs—he is *the best* bass player I've ever seen—[*Snapping back to present.*] Mom! I *know* he's sixteen. Yes, I *know* he can drive. (Duh!) He is not *too cool*. Mom! What does that even mean? You can never be TOO cool! NO one ever died of being TOO COOL! No, I did NOT know he was going to be working when I went to the store. It just so happened that way. When I was leaving we just *happened* to be walking out together and he asked if I wanted to go see if there was a movie playing at AMC, and I was like, "Oh, man, I should call Sarah," but I left my phone at her house and I was like, "Oh, maybe we'll just check out the movie times and then we'll go get her and she'll go too." . . . It was totally logical, but then when we got to the theater, the movie was starting RIGHT THEN, so I had NO choice but to go see *Big Hero 6* RIGHT THEN with Jamie 'cuz he was RIGHT THERE and next thing I know we're licking gummy bears and throwing them at the screen having the time of our lives, laughing our heads off and all of a sudden Bam! Record scratch! YOU, my MOTHER, bust in and take me away—by the arm—and *humiliate* me right then and there in FRONT of Jamie—in front of *JAMIE*, Mom! Without even letting me explain. It was a complete accident. It's obvious! Why don't you believe me? Did you not HEAR my story? Mom! No, Mom, you cannot ground me! I will die! Mom! I have plans on Saturday! Sarah and I have plans. What do you mean, what plans? I already told you about it. Yes I did. We are going to see our friends. It's like, this . . . concert. Just music. Just some friends that we have that are playing music. Their band. Their band is playing music. What are they called? Um . . . Something about hands . . . bracelets, the Furry Chain Bracelets. UGH. Yes! The Fuzzy Handcuffs. UGH! Mom! Why not?! Gaaaaah! [*Big sigh.*] . . . [*Beat.*] . . . Well, then can I at least go spend the night at Sarah's?

Through My Bedroom Window

Daisy Faith

CAROLINE, 14

CAROLINE *is a boy-obsessed psycho who has her own web show. She is setting up her laptop to record another episode of her web show.*

CAROLINE [*Fluffs her hair then presses record.*] Okay. Record.

[CAROLINE *looks through binoculars out of her teenage bedroom window.*]

Good, he's there!

[*She turns to her laptop.*]

A big Redmann High School Rats [*Makes a rat face.*] "hi" to all my obedient viewers for watching Queen Caroline's twenty-eighth episode of [*Gestures with air quotes.*] "Through My Bedroom Window!" New viewers may recognize me from my child starlet days and work in such Lifetime movies as: *Daddy, Where Are You?* and *Papa, May I Play with Danger?* Okay. On today's episode I have a special guest, Brody Bell, spirit fingers [*Wiggles fingers in air with one hand.*], who just got home from the soccer team's away game.

I would have totally been there to cheer my future husband, Brody, on, but because [*Starts to get jealous and dramatic.*] *somebody* named Amanda Mullins claims to have weak wrists (but I just think she's fat and lazy) dropped me when I was on top of the pyramid, I wasn't there. [CAROLINE *starts to weep, and reveals her cast on her broken arm.*]

[*Yelling:*]

Thanks Amanda! Oh, and by the way, I can see your lime-green nail polish from here; it's hideous and it's against cheer guidelines to have any color on your nails other than clear or the approved English Rose . . . [*Yelling.*] Get rid of it! [*Back to cheerful.*] Back to the reason you all tune in every week! Brody! [*Fingers wiggle.*] Spirit fingers!

[*Using binoculars.*] I can see that Brody is playing on his Xbox, O-M-G, it looks like he totally was unpacking because his dirty uniform and boxers are strewn all over the floor. I can see he has a pair with little doggies on them. O-M-G, this is so exciting! And a pair with skull and crossbones, SEXY! I also see a bottle of Hilfiger cologne by Tommy Hilfiger and what appears to be . . . a folded note on his nightstand with the initials BB inscribed on top with two hearts. [*Realization.*] Huh!? O-M-G! That is not my note . . . I haven't written Brody anything in the past three days because I was aware of his travel plans.

[*Devastated, crying.*] I'm sorry, viewers, to get emotional. I know that's totally not appropriate when reporting the news. I'm just a little shocked, because when I was in Brody's room on Saturday on a routine reconnaissance mission, there was no evidence of this note at that present time, which tells me that Brody [*Pathetic wiggle of fingers.*] spirit fingers received this note while at the away game! I'm beginning to smell a rat [*Rat face.*] within the Rat Pack [*Rat face.*] of the cheerleading squad! I want to remind my viewers and especially my fellow squad mates a few things. [*Each point gets heightened with emotion.*] Number one: just because I can't cheer right now [*Shows broken arm in cast.*] doesn't mean I'm not your cheer captain! Number two: when I was six and Brody was seven, we ran naked in the sprinklers *for hours*! It's kismet. He's mine and everybody knows that! And number three: I wrote my name on his ceiling with glow-in-the-dark stars on Saturday and that's way better than some elementary love note! [*An emotional wreck, wiggles fingers lamely.*] Spirit fingers, and thanks for watching another riveting and *surprising* episode of [*Air quotes.*] "Through My Bedroom Window."

[*Mom bursts through her bedroom door.*]

Mom!! Get out! I told you to never interrupt me when I was taping!

Becoming Non-Virgins

Alessandra Rizzotti

RUTH, 16

RUTH *is a total nerd who is jealous that her friend has had sex before her.*

RUTH Remember that time you told me that you were going to stay a virgin until we both decided we wouldn't be virgins anymore? Why did you break that rule, Sarah? You totally disrespected our friendship by having sex with Larry . . . Who cares that you've been together for three years!? I mean I didn't have sex with my Chemistry teacher because he kept putting me in his advance science meet-up groups for the last two years!

Whatever. It's totally the same. I seriously can't believe you and Larry did it while his dog was watching. Talk about not romantic. Didn't you and I agree that we would respect ourselves by making the "act" a spiritual experience with roses and candles in a jade room and shit? I'm not jealous, Sarah. Just annoyed that I don't feel connected to you anymore. It's like you're not my best friend, you know? What do we even have to talk about now? Nothing. Except choir. By the way, did you learn the soprano or mezzo soprano part for *Joseph and the Technicolor Dreamcoat?* The soprano part made me go in my falsetto so I felt like I sounded like an altar boy. Whatever. Who cares anymore? I just don't feel like I have anything in common with you anymore. Now I have to make it my mission to find a boyfriend, date for three years, then have sex.

Sometimes I don't even know if I like boys. Like I knew I loved you because we shared an interest in Ramen, vintage clothes, and ancient art history. But now, I have no idea who I would love, because no one shares those interests. No one. And I'm not filling out a 400-question test on OkCupid just to find out the person that's going to break my cherry. Because why do that? That's too much work.

Tell me, what did it feel like? Was it gross? I don't even want to know. I bet it tasted like Good and Plenties, which are gross. Why do I imagine that? Because, what else would a penis taste like? Himalayan salt crystals? I have no idea because I have no frame of reference. Maybe I should ask my Chem teacher and see if he knows!

Ahhhhhhhhhhhhhhhhhhhh! I'm so sexually frustrated that I started masturbating with a teddy bear I won at the Santa Monica Pier, Sarah. My childhood teddy bear. This means I'm done for. Nobody will want me.

Doesn't Larry have a cousin with Asperger's? Maybe he'll get me. Will you check? Can we still at least go to the cabin this summer and flirt with boys at the lake? Does Larry need to know? Will he care? Ask his cousin to come then. Then we can flirt with our respective possible life partners.

If you don't want to be my friend because you became a non-virgin, then so be it. I'm not going to wait to become a non-virgin just to be your friend. In my mind, you'll always be my friend, Sarah. It's just we'll meet in another lifetime on Mars as aliens or something— because right now, as humans on Earth, we're so not ready to mind-meld and I just don't feel like we'll ever be the same again.

Hey, do you think your mom can pick me up after dance practice today? I won't ask again, don't worry.

This Weekend at Dad's

Braxton Brooks

CHARLIE, 13

CHARLIE *is not a bratty teenager. She is a narcissist, however, due to how deeply embarrassed she is about the situation and her penchant for melodrama. She is in her mom's bedroom, formerly her parents' bedroom.*

CHARLIE   Mo-ooom! This divorce has RUINED my life! I woke up this morning WITH MY FIRST [*Whisper.*] period, and I had to ask Dad to go buy pads because you and TREVOR went away to Napa for the weekend. [*Beat.*]

Aunt Flow came to visit and I had to talk to DAD ABOUT MY [*Whisper.*] period. Which is the worst thing that could happen to a teenage girl! I can't imagine anything worse, can you? Mo-om! It's not funny!

So I wrote out a grocery list and handed it to him while he was watching *CBS Sunday Morning.* I told him it was an emergency, but instead of just going to the store . . . of course he had to read it out loud!

"*People* magazine, Snickers bar, Frosted Flakes, Maxi Pads?"

And THEN do you know what he asked me? Do you know WHAT HE ASKED ME?!

"Charlie, how heavy is your flow? Are you having any menstrual cramps? There's some ibuprofen in the medicine cabinet."

And THEN he went to find a heating pad! I know Dad is a doctor . . . but I don't want to talk to HIM about MY [*Whisper.*] period.

I thought that when I finally got my [*Whisper.*] period, you and me would spend the day together. Because I'm a woman now, Mom. So we'd go get mani-pedis and have brunch and talk about woman stuff, but instead . . . INSTEAD, Dad made me watch him demonstrate how to use "wings" from the comfort of his La-Z-Boy. It was real weird and I'm pretty sure I'm scarred for life.

You don't want me to be scarred for life do you? Puberty is hard enough without having to convince your dad that you don't have to go to the gynecologist yet. No teenage girl should have to discuss the gynecologist with her father!

So here's what I think should happen. First, you should break up with Trevor. He always has coffee breath and he always asks me what my favorite subject is in school. It's Social Studies, TREVOR! It's Social Studies EVERY TIME YOU ASK! Also, if things got more serious . . . you should know the divorce rate for second marriages goes up another 15 percent! Trevor isn't the guy for you.

Second, I'm going to keep getting my [*Mumbles.*] period and other uncomfortable teenage things. So, I think you and Dad should just live together again. At least until I go to college. It would just make things easier for me. Why risk repeating today's tragedy? And studies show that children from two-parent households do better at EVERYTHING! Don't you want me to do better at EVERYTHING?

Mom, if we keep things like they are, I will literally DIE of embarrassment in the next month. Just think how awful you and Dad will feel knowing you could've stopped it from happening.

So, what's it going to be, Mom? Trevor? Or your daughter's life?

Wanted: A Bag of Dry Rice (I Think)

Tiffany E. Babb

JOANIE, 16

JOANIE *is in a bathroom. She looks down directly in front of her.*

JOANIE   Oh. My. God.

[*Pause. Shocked.*]

Nope. Nuh-uh. Nein. This is *not* happening to me. Okay, Joanie. You're okay. Just pick it up out of the toilet.

[*Reaches down and picks the phone up from the floor in front of her, disgusted.*]

Gross. Ew. That is really disgusting. Shoot. Mom is going to murder me. Okay. No problem. I'm just going to have to fix it.

[JOANIE *wipes the phone on her jeans and sets it down gingerly in front of her.*]

How do you fix a wet phone? I know! I'll ask Jessie. She dropped her phone in the pool last year. Let me just call . . .

[*Beat.*]

Okay. Not going to work. Fine, I'll use the Internet. It's the twenty-first century after all. I'll just pull it up on Google. Except for the fact that I have no computer in the bathroom and my phone is covered in pee.

[*Beat.*]

Should I rinse the pee off my phone?

[*Pause.*]

Maybe I'll just slip my phone in my pocket and walk outside and to my laptop. Straight past Mom. She won't notice at all. Except that she will, and then I'll tell her what happened because I am a horrible liar and then she'll kill me with my own pee phone.

[*Beat.*]

What was it that Jessie did anyway? Something with rice, right? Do we have rice in the kitchen?

[*Beat.* JOANIE *wipes her hands on her jeans.*]

[*Sarcastically:*] Hey, Mom. Do you mind going out to the market and buying a bag of rice for me? Why? Oh, no reason. Just make sure you don't cook it?

[*Beat.*]

Or are you supposed to cook it?

[*Beat.*]

Okay. Well, I've got to do something. Or I'll be late for school. Shoot, what time is it?

[JOANIE *reaches for her phone. Realizes that it is dead.*]

I hate my life. Whatever. Alright. I'll just take my phone to school and ask Jessie what to do there. I'm sure someone will have a bag of rice at school for no reason whatsoever.

[JOANIE *pulls her phone out of her pocket and drops it right back into the toilet.*]

Well, shit.

You Call This Punishment?

Andy Goldenberg

KRISTIN, 14

KRISTIN *confronts her teacher during detention.*

KRISTIN   [*Sitting pleasantly, smiling,*] This is fun! Not as exciting as your regular class, but still very entertaining.

[KRISTIN *acts exaggeratedly happy for the satisfaction of her teacher, who is sitting across from her.*]

This is what school should always be like. I'd pay a lot more attention.

[*She smiles at the classroom around her, proud.*] I can sit here all day, Mr. Barretto. All week. I've got an algebra test on Monday, though, so eventually we'll have to make plans to see each other another time.

Sorry. I know. I should be quiet, use this time to study. I just love to talk. Maybe we can catch up during actual class time, or if you're just taking an interest in me, you could always come to one of the color-guard competitions or stalk me online like my parents do.

Oh, come on. You're the one who always gets to talk, talk, talk during class and we don't, and we may as well use this time to get to know one another. I mean, the school system is so overcrowded as it is, I'm surprised you even knew my name when you yelled at me. Yes. Kristin Thatcher. Impressive. Very impressive . . . Michael . . . er, Jason. Peter. No. Fred. Richard. Mister . . . Barretto.

[*She leans in.*] Has anyone ever told you you've got great walls in here? Alex was right. Normally I'm paying too much attention to your lesson plan to let my mind wander, but since I have nothing else to occupy the time, I've really come to appreciate your decor. I honestly really like what you've done with the place. Considering they don't think very highly of social studies and didn't even give you your own classroom. Not that this is horrible, but they could have at least given you air-conditioning. It's practically a ten-minute hike back to the actual campus from the portables, and it's not like you're a teenager anymore. Although my dad wears undershirts more than you do, I guess. Might be something to look into, or maybe lighter colored dress shirts. Maybe it's the fabric. More of a cotton blend? I'm not saying you shop at those cheap discount department stores, but I am saying that if you do, you'll feel so much more confident if you spent just a couple bucks more at a high-end boutique for men. Might stop people from calling you Mr. Bar-sweat-o. I'm sure you already knew that. Right?

[KRISTIN *looks away, toward the walls.*]

Mrs. Leonard has those super lame motivational posters everywhere. You know, the ones with the cats that say stupid things like "Hang in there" and "Purrfect Score" Like purrrr. Like a cat purring. Ugh. So lame.

[*She sits for a beat, smiling.*]

Your form of student torture is never going to break me, Mr. Barretto. I don't need a phone to talk. Obvs. Melissa would crack in less than five minutes without texting somebody. And Allison? Forget it. She'd lose her mind. She'd have to be transferred to Mrs. Shiphead's room down the hall. So it's probably for the best that you singled me out in front of the entire class, even though the two of them were the ones that were actually disrespecting your time. And not to be an A-hole, but, you teach social studies and we were being social. How can you penalize us for that? You should study up on what it means to be our age, 'cause I can't remember the last time I got into a group discussion of some fat president who ruled the country a hundred and fifty years ago. Of course, I'm aiming to be a fashion designer and not some old stuffy librarian who dwells on the past and doesn't even have a Twitter account. That's not you. That's just the image in my head of the kind of people who care about that Taft guy.

But, I'll tell you what. You give me back my phone and I'll Google the dude and tell you exactly what he's known for. Like I said, it won't help me later in life and will probably just get me laughed at, but right here, right now, I don't want to make your life's work seem any less relevant than a bunch of dead people who made some decisions that are super outdated. It's important to know where we came from. I get that. But only if it helps with where we're going.

Here's a homework assignment for you. If you can tell me how Taft changed the face of the fashion world, then maybe I'll be a better student. I'll let you work on that for a little while and I promise to sit here in silence. I'll quietly open my textbook and work on the same thing. We will socially study like the course implies. And I promise to actually attempt to comprehend the words instead of just staring at them, pretending to be reading for twenty-five minutes, like everyone else in class. Deal?

You know, I'm glad this happened, Mr. Barretto. This is fun!

The Great Chili Incident

Katharine McKinney

EMILY, 13 to 15

EMILY *is talking to her best friend in the hallway of her high school.*

EMILY   O-M-G.

You will not believe what just happened to me!

You know that new guy? Kevin? The tall one with the blue eyes who looks like [*Insert name of hot male celebrity here.*]?

Yes. THAT ONE.

I just humiliated myself in front of him forever and now we'll never get married. Yes, of course I think about getting married. No. I don't care that I'm fifteen. Who cares how old I am? I RUINED MY LIFE.

I had the chili at lunch. The chili. What was I thinking? I could have spilled it on my shirt. I could have farted. But what happened was much, much worse.

I was so nervous when he sat right next to me, I didn't know what to do. I started off eating very slowly and delicately, like how I imagine Gwyneth Paltrow eats. I had that peanut butter sandwich and I was just tearing it into small pieces and eating carefully. He just kept talking to the whole group, telling everyone hilarious stories. I got nervous and I started eating faster. By the time I ate the chili I wolfed it down so fast I barely chewed it at all.

Once I ran out of chili I really got nervous. I had a bottled water and started fiddling with it. I picked it up to take a sip just as Kevin started talking about his mom's wig. And I LOST IT. I started laughing so hard, and then I started choking on the water.

And chili came out of my nose.

Chili. Came out. OF MY NOSE.

Chunks of beef. Whole beans. Tomatoes.

Came out of my nose. And landed on Kevin's leg.

It LANDED ON HIS LEG.

Chili came out of my nose and landed on my future husband's leg, only he's not my future husband because now I am a hideous monster who spews disgustingness out of her nostrils.

What do you think I did? I grabbed a napkin and helped him clean it up, and I couldn't even get excited about the fact that I was touching his thigh because of WHY I WAS DOING IT.

Do you think the nurse will send me home now? Because I am dead.

Galaxies Apart

JP Karliak

LINDSAY, 14 to 16

LINDSAY *does well in school, is athletic and artistic, and generally is a motivated, "mature for her age" type of girl who has no time for games. But last night, Andre Carter asked her if she would be his girlfriend. Which means she has a little unfinished business to attend to.*

LINDSAY   [*Shouting offstage.*] I just have to get my track shoes from my room! Could you please make me a sandwich I can take to practice?! Thanks, Mom!

[LINDSAY *shuts the door behind her, stays facing it.*]

Okay. I don't know how long it'll take her to realize I've invaded my brother's room, so I don't have a lot of time. I know it's been forever since we last saw each other, but . . . I had to talk to you.

[*Beat.*]

I'm sorry, it's hard to face you. After all we've been through together, I . . .

[*She turns around. Appears to be looking for someone, who apparently is not there.*]

Wait, where are you?

[*She goes over to a dresser, frantically rummages through a few drawers before withdrawing an action figure. She holds him lovingly.*]

Hey.

You look good, Rigo.

Nah, I think the paint chip adds character. Makes you look distinguished.

Oh, these? [*References her clothes.*] Stop, they're gross, they're just for track. Yeah, definitely not my old Cinderella outfit.

[*She abruptly stands him on the dresser, facing her.*]

No! Turn off the charming, please? This is serious. And I need you to hear me out. I've met someone else.

Well, you couldn't expect that I wouldn't move on. It's been, what, seven years? I'm over it, I'm over you! I'm sure you're over me, I mean . . . you're a prince.

The guy? Oh. Well, his name is Andre. Yeah, he's great—he's editor of the newspaper, cocaptain of the track team with me. He's smart, he's funny, he's really cute . . .

Excuse me? Yes, you are, too, but he's also not eight inches tall!

I'm so sorry, that was rude.

After that fight we had at the end, I've just been holding a lot of resentment. Just seeing you with Strawberry Shortcake like that . . . I dunno. I realize now that, yes, my brother probably put you two in that position—but I was so in love with you then, I couldn't get passed it.

Do you know how much you meant to me? I was suffocating in tea parties with Ken for ages, and he never took me seriously. Never believed I could be anything more than a housewife or a beach volleyball champion like his ex. But then along comes this rugged space prince from the wrong side of the hallway . . . a man who believed I could be anything: a galactic tyrant or even a doctor. I'm applying to premed because of you, did you know that? Sure our love was forbidden, but it was ours. I really believed it would last forever.

Then you met her.

I'll be honest. I think I wanted to tell you about Andre partly because I wanted to hurt you. Or maybe I just wanted some emotion from you about it. Is this affecting you at all? Seriously? Nothing? Ugh, must you always be so stoic and silent? Please just show me you care, Rigo!!

Oh. Oh, I see, *Prince* Rigondrax of Planet Manchego. All business now, huh? Okay. Have it your way. I should have just left you in my brother's underwear drawer. I see that you never really cared. Fine. I'm going. Andre's waiting.

[*She grabs him off the dresser and is about to put him back in the drawer. She sniffs him.*]

Wow. That smell. From when I dyed your hair red with my nail polish.

Prince Rigondrax, I . . . Rigo . . . thank you . . . I'll miss you. I don't think I'll ever love anyone quite the same way.

Here, I'll put you in with his ski gloves. You'll stay nice and warm.

[*She opens up the other drawer. She pauses. And pulls out . . .*]

Strawberry Shortcake?! You're living together!! Oh yeah, "separate rooms," sure!! Ugh, men are pigs! Bye!

[*She throws both into the drawers and storms out.*]

Welcome to U High!

Liz Kenny

TINA BAKER, 13 to 16

In the hallways of University High (U High!)

TINA Hey there. Sarah, right? Welcome to U High!

[*Chanting and fist pumping:*]

U! U! U! High!

That's our school cheer. Wanna try?

[*Pause.*]

Oh, Okay. Maybe some other time. Cool. Cool.

You'll see kids doin' it all the time. Like at a pep rally or something.

Yeah . . . uh . . . I'm Tina Baker. Mrs. Patterson asked me to walk you to class. Sophomore Spanish, right? Senora Kramer is a real bore. Like Senora Snor-a. Ha-ha. You'll see.

Okay. Here is the senior hallway. Okay. Wait. Don't look directly down the hall. It's way not cool. Just . . . take a casual glance down the hall like you didn't even mean to—

[*Flustered.*]

Oh my god. It's Billy Kemper.

Did he see me?
Is he looking at me?

[*Calming down.*]

Okay. Phew!
Billy is in [*Pause for dramatic effect.*] The drumline. You like
drumline? You know, *Ptttttl. Ptttttl. B-rum. Brum. Brum. Brum.
Brum.*

He plays [*Pause for dramatic effect.*] The snare drum.

So just be cool. Be very cool. And walk very cool past this hallway.
Some day, when we're seniors, right? We'll be just cruisin'
together down that hallway.

[TINA *holds up her hand for a high five.*]

Okay. Cool. Maybe on the down low.

[TINA *moves her hand down low.*]

Okay. Not a high fiver. I feel ya.

Mrs. Patterson wanted me to show you the cafeteria in case you
couldn't figure out where everyone was during lunch.

So here it is. The jocks sit outside there. The band sits right
there. And I usually sit here. So you could sit right here next to
me.

Now, see behind the counter there? That's Mrs. Bulgawitz. She is
the best lunch lady. She has so many cool stories about Costco,
and her husband is a office supply salesmen. So they get
unlimited printer ink.

I don't buy my lunch unless it's the fish fry, but if you ever wanna
trade snacks, I've always got homemade garlic beet chips.

[*She reaches for her bag to get some.*]

Oh, okay. Maybe some other time. Cool. Cool.

[TINA *notices something.*]

Oh, wow. Cool phone. Can I have your number? We can like text and stuff.
Oh, okay. Maybe some other time. Cool. Cool.

Well, let's get you next door to Senora Snor-a.

Here we are. La clase de Espanol. Bueno taco or something. I dunno. I parle French.
Hey, uh . . . I know it's hard to be the new kid and make friends and stuff.

I mean, I've been here since day one freshman year and uh . . . still lookin' for my girls. My lady wolf pack, you know? Always down for lady stuff. So if you wanna hang or something. I'd be down.

Oh, okay. Maybe some other time. Cool. Cool.

See ya around, Skeeter!

Like Mother, Like Daughter

Leah Mann

MAKENZIE, 14

A frustrated 14-year-old girl, MAKENZIE, *sits in front of her computer trying to Skype with her mother.*

Mom? Mom! Can you hear me? This connection is bad . . . hang up and try again . . .

[*Beat.*]

Ugh, why is this so difficult?

[*Beat.*]

Mom! Hi! That's way better. You look so tan! Aren't you wearing sunblock? You don't look like you're wearing sunblock. How's Bali? Are you having fun? Did you scuba dive? I really want to scuba dive one day. That's on my bucket list. I wish I was in Bali with you, but I guess that's not how honeymoons work.

[*Beat.*]

And how is Vince? Is HE scuba diving and snorkeling and everything? 'Cause he's not very outdoorsy. It doesn't seem like a great place for him to vacation. I'm not saying he's out of shape or anything. I mean he spends HOW many hours in the gym every day? But he's not much of an adventurer. He doesn't even like spicy foods. Is he eating there? I think he might have an eating disorder. I'm not being mean, but you should keep an eye on him because I'm not sure about the health of his psyche. But you know that, I shared all my concerns with you before the wedding and that didn't change your mind. The hearts wants what the heart wants. That's what Grandma always says and she's very smart. Your heart wants Vince. I support that, even though he's "not a kid person" and you have three kids, which seems kind of like a deal breaker to me, but as he said at the wedding, he "loves you even though you come with so much baggage." And you love him.

[*Beat.*]

Dad's fine, by the way. Not that you asked. Hannah and Mike are staying with him all week because he was sad. I mean, he's fine, but he's sad. It's hard for him, I think, with you away and having a fun, exotic honeymoon and doing lots of—whatever stuff you do—with your new husband on a honeymoon while he's alone in his tiny house. He went on a date, but she was pretty mean to him. Plus the cat is sick and keeps puking everywhere, which smells super bad. Did you know the cat was sick? You haven't asked about her, is why I ask, and she was your cat first.

[*Beat.*]

I never said you're horrible! How was I supposed to know you're paying the vet bills? Don't put words in my mouth. I hate when you do that. You don't know what I'm thinking.

[*Beat.*]

I'm not mad at you.

[*Beat.*]

Maybe I'm a little mad at you . . . Of course I want you to be happy, I love you, you're my mom, you should be happy . . . But Vince!?!?! Gross.

[*Beat.*]

Ew, Mom, ew. I know, on like, an intellectual level that you're a woman with . . . needs . . . but don't make me think about it in real life, like in practice or whatever. You want your kids thinking about you . . . doing it?

[*Beat.*]

It is NOT healthy! It's weird. You're being weird. You're a mom. I'm a kid. I'm not going to make you think about all the sex stuff that I do. You don't want to think about that even though I'm also a woman with needs.

[*Beat.*]

I am TOO a woman. I got my period, remember? Oh, right, you were busy working on the seating chart for the reception and Dad had to buy me pads until you had time to try to explain tampons to me. That makes me just as much of a woman as you. Maybe I'll find a Vince and run away from my family to have sex on the beach and get tan even though we have a family history of melanoma and Dad is a dermatologist who forwards articles about sunblock and cancer like every ten minutes.

[*Beat.*]

I'm glad you're wearing sunblock.

[*Beat.*]

Yes, you look super hot and relaxed.

[*Beat. She waves wanly.*]

Hi Vince.

[*Beat.*]

Yes, Mom. Vince also looks hot and relaxed.

[*Beat.*]

I'm almost done with them. I don't know why you're making me do all your thank-you cards. I don't think the punishment fits the crime. All I did was give you guys gluten. How was I supposed to know that Vince is part of the one percent of the population that legitimately has celiac disease?

[*Beat.*]

I SAID I was sorry. I'm not just SAYING it—I mean it. Just because I think Vince is a total tool doesn't mean I want him getting super sick and shitting your entire wedding night. I still don't think that justifies forging three hundred thank-you cards in your handwriting. Do you know how hard your handwriting is to copy? I mean, who writes cursive anymore? Can't I just e-mail them or do like a Facebook message?

[*Beat.*]

Yeah-yeah, Miss Manners, I get it. Gestures are important and it's polite. Ugh.

[*Beat.*]

Oh, so sorry to keep you from your elephant ride. Please, excuse me for wanting to talk to my mom who I love and miss and is on the other side of the world. I'll stop bugging you with my life.

[*Beat.*]

Love you too! Totally just said that. Go have more fun with your . . . [*Sighs.*] husband. I'll get back to the thank-you cards. They'll be done before you're back in two days.

[*Beat.*]

You're extending your trip?

[*Beat.*]

Until my attitude improves?

[*Beat.*]

I get my attitude from you, so I wouldn't hold your breath. You maybe want to apply for dual citizenship, because I'm not making any promises. Grandma says the apple doesn't fall far from the tree and you're the rough, crinkly old tree and I'm the shiny red apple!

[*Beat.*]

Will you bring me back a present?

[*Beat.*]

Not a little brother or sister! God, Mom—haven't you hit menopause yet? Gross. Is that Vince's butt? Why is he naked? How hard is it to wear a towel? Doesn't he know what FaceTime is?

Bye, already.

Mommy Dearest

Alisha Gaddis

ROSE, 12 to 15

ROSE *is in bed with her mom, which we find out later. Her mother is an alcoholic and* ROSE *is in a highly dysfunctional codependent relationship.*

ROSE   Scoot over! Please scoot over. Your feet are freezing and they are touching me! Can you please get on your side of the bed? Puh-leez.

[*Beat.*]

When are you going to turn off *Desperate Housewives*? You know you shouldn't be watching that. It is bad for your brain and I have a math test tomorrow—and if it is on then it is actually affecting *my* brain and I need all the help I can get with fractions. I don't need to hear two grown ladies screaming about whose noses are fake. I mean—we all know Louisa's is—for sure!

Can you at least turn it down?

[*Beat.*]

Are you eating Cheetos in bed again?! Gah-ross. You know that orange dust gets all over the sheets and your fingers. Last time you fell asleep watching *Downton Abbey* and there were flecks all over your mouth and there were pieces crushed into the crevices of your neck. That is just not cute.

GET YOUR FEET OFF ME PLEASE! THEY ARE COLD!!

Do you have the alarm set? Are you sure? This will be the third time this week that it accidentally doesn't go off. iPhones don't do that. They don't accidentally not work because of a world clock time change three times in a row. I Googled it. You have to get up on time—we cannot be late.

YOUR TOES ARE TOUCHING ME AGAIN!

Listen, do you have your clothes picked out for tomorrow—or do you need me to help you again? You have to stop wearing those tacky scarves and butterfly clips. They are not cute in a retro way yet. Thanks for helping me with my outfit. I can't wait to see what you picked!

[*Beat.*]

You are laughing so loudly! Nana is going to hear you! That Geiko commercial is not that funny! Can we please get some rest—it is past midnight! I am developing bags under my eyes at the very young age of fifteen! [*To self.*] I need to get a cream for that.

Mom—I think this is really the last time I can sleep and cuddle with you again. You need to start sleeping in your bed by yourself. Or at least get a boyfriend.

[*Beat.*]

I KNOW I am better than a boyfriend. And yeah—I AM your best friend. I KNOW you want to take me to get a tattoo that says we are, but Dad won't let me yet. I agree—that is stupid. I totally want a matching BFF tattoo with you, Mom. That is not what I am saying. But this is getting weird. I am not six anymore. I have my own room and my own bed and so do you and we need to start using them. I am going to have a boyfriend soon too. I mean, everyone else in the whole high school does. I don't really know why I don't. I mean, people say I am kinda weird and clingy—and when I found out that Trey liked me last year, I just thought it was totally normal to cut his food for him at lunch and wait for him outside of the bathroom to dry his hands after he hopefully washes them when he pees—just like you do for me!

People think it is weird that I still kiss you and Nana and Grandpa on the mouth. I mean, it is only semi-open with no tongue. That is not gross at all! It is totally European!

But I want to open-mouth kiss a boy, Mom—with the tongue. Not just Mustard my stuffed animal.

Candice at school also said it is weird that we all live kinda in a compound. Like the whole family lives together or within super close distance, and no one goes to college we just educate our own because we know best and we have to stick together. Just like you told me.

YOUR TOES MOM—THEY ARE COLD!!!

But maybe . . . Maybe . . . I want to go to my own room and live my own life and move to New York City and own an art gallery and live my dreams! Maybe I want to shampoo my own hair and tie my own shoes and be me!!!!

[*Beat.*]

Mom, are you crying? . . . Mama? . . .

Don't cry.

Oh. Robin just slapped Taylor? Woah. Didn't see that coming.

Let me go get us some ice cream to go with those Cheetos and we can snuggle in for a little bit. Maybe you should reset the alarm. I wanna see this and I don't have to be THAT on time for school.

Do you want me to get you some socks for your cold piggies?

[*Beat.*]

Love you too, Mommy Dearest.

Poem

Alessandra Rizzotti

OLIVIA, 14

OLIVIA *gets on stage to recite a poem for the middle school talent show. She's nervous.*

OLIVIA   My name is Olivia Eloise. Entering in the alternative section of the talent show, reading my original poetry, typed on a Mac computer in study break, within ten minutes. So here goes.

"Confession"

I wasn't going to say it
But I'm doing it
Here right now
You are my everything
I love how you express yourself
In watercolor class
Or how you cradle flour babies in home ec
You're like the sun to my moon
The "can" in my "cannot"
The rainbow in my clear crystal
My best friend
My crush/crushed ice
The cool rain in my heat wave
I would pick all the flowers in the world for you
So what I'm about to say may seem surprising

Or totally obvious
Probably obvious
Since I told you in a frog-shaped Post-it note one time
That
I like you
Will you go to the school dance with me, Adina?
We can dress like anime characters

[OLIVIA *stops, closing her eyes, afraid of the outcome.*]

[*Whispering to herself.*] Please say yes please say yes please say yes.

[OLIVIA *opens her eyes slowly, squinting, trying to not look at the crowd, then starts to smile.*]

Oh man. Adina! That's the coolest "YES" I've ever seen! How did you guys get together and do that so fast? Cheerleaders. Ha-ha. Ha-ha. So cool. *Y*—is that a "3"?—kidding. And an *S*! Charlie's arms and legs look so uncomfortable. You don't have to hold it anymore, guys. I got the message! I can't believe you did that!

My gratitude
Is boundless
For your friendship

[OLIVIA *bows and thanks them, hands to heart.*]

You won't regret this, Adina. I bought the coolest tux so that you can do your girly Forever 21 thing.

[OLIVIA *turns her head as if she's been interrupted.*]

Yes, Mrs. Franken, that was it. I don't care if I'm disqualified! I was using the stage to ask Adina out and she said YESSSS!

Weeee! Best day ever! Adina, so, like, want to go get Slurpees after this? Or shall I say . . .

I made cookies
In the shape of stars
Because you are one
Let's share them

[OLIVIA *turns her head as if she's been interrupted.*]

Mrs. Franken, you're lame. Teen love is in the air!

[OLIVIA *puts a "stop" hand motion towards Mrs. Franken and turns her head the other way, breathing in.*]

Step off
The boat of love
You are not welcome

[*She takes a moment to compose herself, then . . .*]

Come on Adina, we're not welcome here. As always. You'd think a Waldorf school would UNDERSTAND, but they're not THERE yet.

[OLIVIA *stomps off, shouting.*]

We're here! We're queer! Black lives matter!

I know you're not black, Adina. But, I'm a quarter, so it counts. Have a blessed day, Mrs. Franken!

Designer Jeans

Daisy Faith

MARGO, 13 to 15

MARGO *confronts her mom about her designer jeans at the local hip store in the mall.*

MARGO Don't get it twisted, Mom—take your Zoloft and schedule a spa appointment! Yes, I bought a pair of $400 stone-washed jeans from Australia, and thanks for just looking at my private receipts—I told you when it's on the floor, it's off-limits! This is why I hate living in this domestic prison—it's like a suburban straightjacket. Mom, what did you do with the box the jeans came in? Please tell me you did not throw away the box—it had a picture of a kangaroo on it—without the packaging these jeans are like totally worthless. Yeah, you better find it! You better hope the recycling hasn't been picked up! They're not just tattered, they're custom—I had to take the pair of denim jeans and wash them with the provided pumice stones in the washer, and then you take a customized eucalyptus razor blade and rip them and cut them to look like the diagram. And news flash—I did not break the washer, it was already acting depressed. No, Mom—stop freaking out, you don't need to cut yourself over this. You don't get it—that's why it's so expensive, because it is DIY—do it yourself!

O-M-G, how many times have I tweeted that I want to work in fashion—no one is going to take me seriously if I don't look hip and cutting edge. You know my motto. Number one: buy it. Number two: wear it. Number three: be it. Miley Cyrus was just seen wearing a pair of these in *Us Weekly*, so you know this trend is gonna last! It's going to be like Uggs—we just can't get rid of them, they're like a virus infecting ankles worldwide. No, Mom— not like crocs, crocs are so over! You should be grateful like a bimbo is to her sugar daddy, because I'm on my way to being like a freakin' fashion mogul you might want to get in on the ground floor. And if you want to be involved in my fashion empire, you better stop wearing that ridonkulous pink Juicy sweat suit—that's so J.Lo circa 2002!

No, Mom, I don't need to study . . . style can't be taught! I'm currently reviewing potential investors, on your computer, so don't touch it. And take that embarrassment off!! You look like a pink Peep! You know that's got to be why Dad left you!

The Job Interview

Rachel Pollon

EMMA BANKS, 15 to 18

EMMA *sits on a folding chair in front of a messy desk across from her interviewer in a florescent-lit makeshift office space in the back room of an ice-cream shop.*

EMMA   Well, first off I just want to thank you again. I'm sure you must have a lot of qualified candidates lined up to interview for the job, and I appreciate that you saw something promising enough in my resume for you to meet with me.

As for what qualifies me for the position?

The most obvious thing is that I love ice cream. I mean, not obvious because I'm fat, I'm obviously of a normal weight . . . not that there would be anything wrong with it if I had a few extra pounds on me. I think society puts too much pressure on us to be perfect-slash-unnaturally skinny. I mean—for all you know, I purge!

I don't purge.
And I don't binge.

I would not sneak ice cream if you hired me to work here. You can ask anyone on my reference list—I am super honest. Too honest, they might say. Shut up, they might also say, you never know when to stop talking!

I've gotten off track.

I love ice cream, in a completely normal way that non-lactose-intolerant people love ice cream.

Speaking of which, do you have any lactose-free products? I know lots of people who would like that. My Nana, especially. I mean she lives in New Hampshire, but if she were ever to visit, I would love for her to be able to come witness me behind the counter at work and be able to offer her a treat.

But that probably isn't too important since she rarely travels and when we do see her, which isn't often because my mom and her kind of fight a lot, we go to her.

Anyway, what other things should you know about me?

I am punctual. That was also the name of a quote-unquote punk band I was in for three weeks last summer—Punktual. Get it?

I'm not an anarchist, by the way, just because I was in a punk band. It was only three weeks. I played tambourine.

What else . . .

I love people. Love them. I am overly nice. More than one person has urged me to grow a backbone and say no every once in a while.

Speaking of saying no, I definitely say no to drugs . . . I have gotten a contact high a couple of times without realizing it when hanging out in my older brother's bedroom while some friends of his were smoking, but that doesn't count, right? I tell you what though, ice cream tasted really good on those days.

You know what? I'm going to stop now and let you do the talking.

Anything else you want to ask me?

Anyway, It's Mom's Wedding . . .

Charity L. Miller

CONNIE, 13 to 17

CONNIE *is at the wedding reception of her mom.*

CONNIE Attention, everybody! Attention . . . I would tap on a glass or a bottle, but Uncle Theo keeps taking them from my hands. *I'm not trying to drink, Uncle Theo. I'm not stupid, okay.* The first rule of underage drinking is to NOT get wasted with your mom, like, fifty feet away. Duh!

Anyway, can I please get everybody's attention and stuff? As the eldest daughter of the bride, slash, maid of honor, I just wanted to take a moment to make a toast to my hero and the real reason we are all here tonight. I know it's Mom's fourth wedding and stuff and I am really Kanye happy for her and all, but I really *needed* to give a much-needed and much-deserved shout-out to the super stellar rock star of tonight's festivities. *Oh, my god! Aunt Karen, sit down! Today is like, totes, not about you!*

Any which, I'm talking about Grandma right now. [*Beat.*] This is the part where you people clap and stuff. [*Beat.*] Thank you. Ugh. My grandma made . . . *Aunt Karen! Stop crying! You're ruining my speech!* My grandma made a lot of sacrifices for my mom to get married. [*Beat.*] Wait. No. I'm not talking about the whole sixth grade Sex Ed part, but like the true sacrifices that Grandma made in order for me, I mean Mom, to be happy.

Any what, Grandpa Joseph died in the Great War . . . Vietnam. Everyone knows that Grandma was a single mother who worked six jobs to feed and clothe her four children. [*Beat.*] What? Two jobs? Whatever, that's still a lot of jobs for one grandma to work. Any who, Mom never knew Grandpa Joseph, because he died before she was born. And according to Grandma, that is why Mom is like Elizabeth Taylor—always marrying random dudes to fill the void left by never knowing her father. When Mom met Rodney, I was like, "Ew." But then Grandma made me realize that older people have different standards of what they look for in a BF, and that is stuff like paying taxes and being a manager at their job. Grandma was the one that made me realize that unlike strong, independent women like me, Rihanna, and Grandma, moms can feel alone and sad and that's why men like Rodney and websites like OurTime.com exist.

OH MY GOD, AUNT KAREN! WILL. YOU. STOP!?! Anyhow, thanks to Grandma's guidance and tutelage, I was able to grant Rodney and Mom my blessing. Even though they originally wanted to have a boring old people's wedding at the courthouse, Grandma convinced me that by not pouting and throwing a fit, I would be able to get the wedding of my, I mean, Mom's dreams.

Any why, Grandma was the one that listened to me when I was mad that Mom wanted me to move into Rodney's house because his house was bigger than our house. Grandma reminded me that I would get my own room and that we could finally have a dog because Rodney loves dogs. Rodney has three dogs. Although I'm happy that he rescued them, three dogs is too many dogs for one single man to have. He claims that they were his ex-wife's, but

Grandma said Rodney used dogs like Mom used men to fill the void of being old and alone in a giant house without love.

Any which, Grandma said that if I change my outlook about Rodney and "focus on finding my happy, I would be at peace with it." She was right. Grandma is always right. Mom was really pissed when I painted my new room black. But Grandma was the one that told Mom, "Remember when you dyed your hair purple and went through that phase where you only listened to The Cure?" Then Mom was like, "Oh my god, Mom. You're right. I'm so sorry, Connie. You can paint your room black."

Any how, Grandma was the one who helped Mom pick out her wedding dress. Mom couldn't decide on which dress to choose and I had a migraine because we totally looked at like fifteen dresses in a six-hour time span and I was like, "Oh my god, I'm going to puke all over David's Bridal!" And then Grandma was like, "What about this dress, sweetie?" and it was the perfect dress for Mom. I personally thought the dress was super ugly and would have killed myself if it was for my wedding, but Mom LOVED the dress. Even though it showed too much cleavage for Grandma's liking, it covered Mom's knees so there was a classy balance (which is really important to older people like Grandma). When Grandma grew up in the 1960s, women weren't allowed to drink or show their ankles. So modesty was super important to them.

Any way, Mom loved the dress and only needed one alteration to make it fit her booty. Grandma always knows the perfect dress for Mom and for my prom and even for Aunt Karen's employee-of-the-month luncheon and Cousin Skooter's funeral. Skooter looked so beautiful in her casket thanks to Grandma.

Tonight is a special night for Mom and Rodney and even for Aunt Karen who had to walk Mom down the aisle since Grandpa Joseph died a long, long, long time ago, like the 1980s. [*Beat.*] *The '70s?! That's even older.* Ew.

Anyway. I just wanted to let everyone know how great Grandma was and how awesome today is because of her. I only wish Grandma could be here tonight to see how right she was about everything. About how pretty Mom looks in her dress. How happy Rodney looks sitting next to Mom. How Aunt Karen can't ever stop being so freaking dramatic. *Like, seriously . . . Aunt Karen!*

And Grandma said I would be able to say my entire speech without crying. And I did. I didn't cry once. [*Cries.*] I miss Grandma a lot. Sometimes when people tell me I have a nice smile, I think of Grandma. We have the same smile. My mom also has that same smile. And for a long time, my mom never smiled, because she was sad that my dad cheated on her with the school nurse.

But one day Grandma said that Mom should take a chance on Rodney. And Mom did. And Rodney took my mom to Sizzler and he even let her get a salad. And Mom came home and she was smiling. And I was smiling because Mom was smiling. And Grandma was smiling because me and Mom were smiling. So, tonight I want to give a toast to my grandma. Because without my grandma, Mom and Rodney wouldn't be happy together forever. And I wouldn't have my own room. [*Beat.*] I know Grandma is smiling down from her top prison bunk and she's proud of us all. I love you, Grandma!

Of Mini Tigers

Lauren Candia

SOPHIE, 15

SOPHIE *is in a public library. She arrives at the checkout counter with a stack of books and a dazed look on her face.*

SOPHIE   How am I doing? Oh, fine. Just being plagued by mini tigers. I'm talking about my [*Whispers.*] period.

I hated the idea of being a late bloomer, but I had no idea how lucky I was. I'm thinking about all the times I went to people, "When am I going to get mine? When is it going to happen?"

And then all the sympathy, "Oh, it'll come. It's totally normal. Your body is fine."

So clueless. I didn't realize it wasn't sympathy that I needed. I needed a plan to disguise my uterus and smuggle it out of the country.

Because if I can just real talk for a second . . . my body feels anything but fine right now. It feels like I'm being eaten alive by mini tigers from the inside out. Totally not fine. And I knew this was coming. It's not like nobody told me this experience would be painful. How many times have I seen my friends doubled over with cramps and secretly wished we could be sisters in misery together?

There's just no preparing for mini tigers.

But what's really getting to me . . . what really, really just burns me up inside . . . is that I can't talk about it. It's like . . . I'm going through this thing . . . half the world is going through this thing . . . but I'm not supposed to mention the mini tigers. I'm supposed to keep it all to myself and not complain and act like nothing is wrong? That's so stupid.

If I had things my way, the first thing people would know about me after saying hi is that I'm on my period. Then maybe I wouldn't have to apologize for not being funner, and maybe someone would take pity and give me chocolate.

So, feel free to pile on the sympathy. It's too late. The cycle is in motion. I guess for the sake of not making everyone uncomfortable, I won't go on too long about this, but I'm just saying . . . my vagina hurts.

So anyways, do you still need my library card?

Manic Pixie Dream Girl

Carla Cackowski

PILAR, 18

PILAR *speaks to her YouTube fans with an intimacy usually reserved for close friends and family. She is part Lolita, part Tinker Bell—both infuriating and magical. In her most vulnerable moments, both men and women find themselves under her spell. PILAR arranges herself in a chair until she feels cute and comfy. A computer screen is open in front of her. She presses the record button on the keypad.*

PILAR   Hi, YouTube friends. Pilar here. It's been a few hours since I last vlogged. I missed you. I love you. I hope you love me too.

I wanted to give a quick shout-out to Jacob. Jacob left a comment on my page saying, "You are the girl of my dreams." To Jacob I respond, "Thank you. You are one of the men in my dreams."

I received another comment, this time from a *female*. Nancy says, "Pilar, I feel like I know mostly everything about you. So tell us, what's inside of your purse?"

It's true, Nancy, I've shown you so much of my insides, my truth, my essence, but never the inside of my purse. So today, my friends, my lovers, my confidants—today I'm going to show you the inside of my most intimate object. I call it my Mary Poppins purse.

[PILAR *giggles like a little girl as she opens a purse as large as a piece of luggage. As she describes each object, she holds them preciously in her hands as though she were unearthing a buried treasure.*]

The first thing I have is a journal. This is where I keep my most private thoughts . . . I've read all of it to you in previous vlogs.

Next: lip balm. This is my favorite brand of lip balm. It keeps my lips moist so that my secrets spill out easily.

I always carry a pair of panties. Not just any panties, but my lucky panties. I never leave home without them. They're like magic fairy dust, granting the wishes of every human they come into contact with. I've never actually worn them, because I don't wear panties, but I'm so relieved to have them with me when the universe presents obstacles that try to block my happy path.

And finally, my Bobbi Brown eye liner and a picture of Gandhi.

[PILAR *kisses the picture.*]

So there you have it, Nancy . . . the inside of my purse. Maybe next time I'll show you the inside of my throat. I think it's pretty rad.

This afternoon, while I was planning what I was going to say about myself, I decided to pose for a new profile pic.

[PILAR *presses a button on her computer to show the audience her picture.*]

I think this outfit is okay, but what I really love about this picture is my skinny face. I like it so much that it inspired an idea for a contest! Send me the best skinny face picture of yourself and I'll pick a winner. That person will be sent the name and address of my gynecologist so you can get a pap by the same man's hands that gave me my pap. I like to promote women's health issues

when I can. That's why I dyed my hair pink this morning . . .
because Breast Cancer Awareness month was a few months ago.

So, now I'd like to talk to you about something uber personal.
Should I talk about it? I don't know, maybe I shouldn't. Should I?
I don't know. I can't. But I have to! I must!

[PILAR *channels Lolita.*]

Turns out someone came into possession of a sex tape I made
with my boyfriend three boyfriends ago and posted it on
YouTube. I feel so violated. Like, that sex tape was for us, not for
the public. Because when two people love each other, the best
way for them to express it is to put a camera on a tripod and tape
their most intimate moments. It got 1.4 million unique views and
made the YouTube top 10! I feel so depressed about this whole
incident. I've lost my appetite and won't be able to eat at my
favorite restaurant, Jamba Juice, for, like, days.

[*And then, Tinker Bell!*]

Let's go on an adventure! Let's break into houses that aren't ours!
Let's splash our naked feet in Trevi Fountain while singing a
Shins song! Let's stand in front of Tiffany's eating ice cream and
call it breakfast! Let's do it!

[PILAR *sighs like, "It's so hard to be* PILAR.*"*]

I hope you feel like you've gotten to know me better over the past
few minutes. I definitely feel like I've gotten to know you, you
marvelous human beings, you.

[PILAR *blows a kiss to her audience and closes the computer.*]

Hashtag ZanderInOurHeartsForever

Orly Minazad

PIPER, 14

PIPER *is hanging out on her bed, empty Starbucks drink in hand, video chatting with her cousin, around the same age, about Zander Goodhair leaving One Dimension, her favorite boy band.*

NOTE: The symbol "#" is to be read as "hashtag."

PIPER   You wouldn't believe this. Nora Snapchatted me in middle of Mr. Parker's class with her face covered in tears. Why would she Snapchat me? We haven't spoken since like the fifth grade, when she got super annoying after getting over three hundred likes on a hairstyle she posted on Instagram #PleaseStop #GetOverYourself. Anyway, if she took time away from her famousness to talk to me, I knew it was for real. Then I read the caption, "Zander broke up w 1D!!!" ☹

It was a week before April Fool's Day but I was pretty sure it was an April Fool's prank, right? Zander leaving One Dimension? #NotCool #TheWorst #MyHeartBleeds.

But it was true. It was even on old-people channel CNN, so obvsi it's true. We hugged and cried together later because, you know, tragedy brings people together. Even me and #CrazyNotInAGoodWay Nora.

Rumor has it that he's leaving to be a "normal twenty-two-year-old." #ImNotThatStupid. That Carnival cruise ship has sailed, Zan! What do you think is going to happen? We'll run into you picking up your dry cleaning and be like, "Oh that's Zander Goodhair. He used to be in One Dimension, one of the greatest boy bands in the world, *but now he's normal like the rest of us so let's leave him alone*." #NotGonnaHappen #WeDeserveTheTruth.

Yeah, it's been a tough day. I can't sleep, I can't eat, I can't Instagram. There's a whole world right now that doesn't know I got a Birthday Cake Frappuccino #StarbuckSecretMenu to cheer me up. But it didn't work. I just sat on my bed, alone like some crazy lonely person with my headphones, listening to One Dimension's "Hey Gurl Let's Chill" #ThatsMyJam and wondering what went wrong. What could we have done differently? Is it our fault? Did we love too much? Not enough? #ZanComeBack #1DForEverWithYou.

Yes, I told Mom the news when I got home after school because I thought she'd be supportive like a normal mom.

No, she just said, "Don't leave your socks on the floor. How many times am I supposed to tell you?"

"Mom, did you not hear me. *Zander Goodhair left*?"

"Who's that? Your math teacher?"

#EyeRoll

I explained everything to her. Which turned out to be more complicated than explaining to her what emojis are #40YearOlds. I told her about Zan's charm, and tattoos bringing meaning to my existence. His voice like smooth, in-season strawberry froyo topped with cookie dough bits and marshmallow sauce comforting me when I needed it most. O-M-G, that should totally be a Starbucks secret recipe #IdeasThatMatter.

Anyway, she went off on her usual "I didn't immigrate to this country after living through the Islamic Revolution so you can waste your time crying over some guy in a kiddie band who doesn't even care or know you exist" lecture. You know what, Mom? *#TheStruggleIsReal and the revolution happened like a million years ago so #GetOverIt. The only revolution that matters right now is the one happening in my heart! #PleaseZanComeBack.*

"Stop being a drama queen. It's not like he's dead. He's probably just going solo blah blah blah," she says.

I made a mental note to report her to social services. I'm sure this is considered child abuse.

Does she think Zan going solo makes all this better? He can't go solo. They're called ONE Dimension. Not TWO. It's like parents separating and telling their kids that they're "going solo" and you being like, "Oh, it's cool. *Not like you're dying or anything.*" I know, because when her and Dad divorced, nothing was ever the same again. I can't split my time and attention between the two. No, not Mom and Dad. I mean One Dimension and whatever Zan will be doing. Eventually, I'll prefer one over the other. And that's not fair to either.

It was in the middle of Mom's "You're going to high school next fall so it's time you get serious about life and probably get one of those rolling backpacks" lecture when I suddenly had an epiphany. Well, first I had to Google "epiphany" to make sure that's what I was having and it wasn't just a major sugar rush from the multiple Frappuccinos. Yes, I'm totally having "a sudden, intuitive perception of or insight into the reality or essential meaning of something, usually initiated by some simple, homely, or commonplace occurrence or experience" #NailedIt.

Sure, it seems crazy to obsess over musicians that never follow you on Instagram no matter how many times you ask them to #FolloBackForFolloBack, but every generation has a Zander Goodhair or a Jerry Abssteel or a Lionel Sidebangs. Mom lost her mind when some old dudes in their thirties called N'Sane had a reunion at the MTV Music Awards for a few seconds. So why can't she understand my struggle.

More than his scruffy boy-man beard and his mysterious eyes, I had a connection with Zan and his profound wisdom, most of which are tattooed on his body—probably so he doesn't forget them. Like "Be true to who you are" and "All right chlamydia boy" (which I'm yet to figure out what it means) and my favorite, "Just close your eyes and enjoy the roller coaster that is life." I'd like to think he's speaking directly to me and our journeys ahead, mine to high school and his to wherever—maybe underwear model, reality star, or a colab with Niki Minaj #YesPlease #ZanInOurHeartsForever.

No Time for Cults

Kayla Cagan

ABBY, 15 to 16

ABBY, *at the food court in a mall, addresses the cult members who are waiting to hear if she will join them or not.*

ABBY Thanks for meeting me in the food court today. I thought it would kind of be nice here, since this is where we first met. [*Pause.*] You're probably wondering if I have an answer for you. Well, I do.

After a lot of careful consideration and thought, and you guys have to know this was like, super-duper hard for me, I don't think I can join your cult. I know, I know—before you say anything, Donald, I know how much you guys think I would be perfect for your whole deal. But to be honest, I'm not like, perfect. I know. It is hard to believe. I agree. But here are some things I don't think you know about me.

One. I don't think I'm going to be good about giving up makeup and hairspray and like, living the rest of my life with a ponytail. I mean I can rock a pony, don't get me wrong, and my top knot is on point, but the whole never ever getting a blowout again business? I dunno, guys. Kind of like phoney baloney, you know what I mean?

Two. I just got my learner's permit. Do you even know what that means? That means I'm about to drive, and yes, it's just sharing my mom's Kia Sportage, but that's like total freedom. And the idea of not getting behind the wheel right when I'm like, legal? C'mon. Would you give up your car . . . even if it was a Sportage? Well, I guess that's a dumb question because you've all already given up all your cars, but I just don't think I can. And besides, my mom would kill me if I told her the truth. "Like, Hey Mom! You know how much you love your heated seats? Well, no more, Mamacita! You're walking in the freezing cold because I had to give your car away!" You guys, she would be so pissed at me. She's loves her freaking Sportage. Trust me.

And . . . three. Rooftop just asked me out. I know what you're thinking: that I'm smarter and better than Rooftop. Everyone says that, I know I know—but like he's the best skater at our school and he has the hottest abs. No offense, but all of you guys wear dresses that look like they are made of old bedsheets, and that's not really my thing. I've been perfecting my look since I was twelve, and I kind of want the guy I date to look hot, too. Rooftop is like, everything. He's major. You get it, right?

So, even though I hate saying no, especially when you guys have been so nice to me, I'm just going to have to say it. I don't have time for your cult right now, but I totally appreciate it, You Cuties. Maybe in a few years. But right now? No thanks.

Hate to "break up" and run, but I promised to meet Rooftop at Hot Topic because they're having a sale on T-shirts, and he like, totally needs a refresh. See ya—and good luck with all your cult stuff!

[ABBY *waves and runs off quickly.*]

The Red Badge of Courage

Sarah McChesney

SANDY MCDERMOTT, 13

SANDY is at Allison Park Middle School Auditorium addressing her classmates.

SANDY   Dear esteemed peers,

Good afternoon, as you know my name is Sandy McDermott, your student council president. Today is a big day for us eighth graders, as it is our last day at Allison Park Middle School. Next year we will be at Allison Park High School, a new school with new teachers and new beginnings. Our mascot will still be The Owls, FYI.

Since we are beginning our journey into adulthood, I would like to take this time to talk to you, my esteemed peers, about how we should behave next year in high school.

In middle school, we joke and laugh and make fun of each other and that's okay because we're kids. But in high school we won't do this any more because we'll pretty much be adults. The bullies at this school have made fun of lots of us, like Nittan Mishravi, because he's eight and should be in elementary school but he's Indian so he's super smart; Gayle Strizinger, because her dad works at Burger King and we don't know who her mom is; and

Becky Rollins, because she tried out for band and didn't get in, which everyone knows is super easy. But I'm not going to use those guys as examples, because that wouldn't be fair. So instead I'm going to do something very hard and use myself.

Earlier in the school year, I was in Mrs. Russell's second period math class. It was the week we were learning Perimeter and Circumference, which was pretty cool. If Mrs. Russell is here, I'd like to give her a shout-out because she really knows how to teach Geometry. Anyway, I wasn't feeling well that day; my stomach hurt and I just felt crappy. Excuse my language, Principle Maloney. When the bell rang, I got up to leave and I realized that it was . . . "that time of the month." If you guys don't know what that means, it's menstruation.

I didn't want to get up because I was wearing my favorite American Eagle light-wash skinny jeans and there was no way it hadn't leaked and I didn't want any of you guys to see so I waited until you all left. Sorry Greg, I know I told you I was looking for a super interesting math problem that I had just thought of, but that was a lie. I had actually thought of one the day before.

After everyone left I grabbed my books and tried to get to Mr. Fisher's English class as fast as possible. I figured if I could get there, then I could ask to borrow Alison Moroziak's navy-blue Gap cardigan, to tie around my waist . . . you guys know, the one she always wears on Thursdays. I was almost there, like super close, but then I heard the worst noise ever. It was John Glock, Matt Jacobs, and Chad Drodz walking up behind me being all loud and stuff. I know you guys know this, but I have to say it. Those guys are jerks. I'm sorry, Principle Maloney, but it's true. They are just like hyenas—hyenas are basically the jerks of the animal kingdom, and I know this because I watch *Nature* on PBS with my dad.

I was hoping *so bad* that those guys wouldn't see me, I know it's not possible but I was seriously trying to be invisible. But then John Glock yelled "She got her period!" and then Matt and Chad kept laughing and whispering and then they spread it all over the school and even the teachers knew because Mrs. Kopiak the school nurse tried to talk to me about tampons vs. pads. Embarrassing.

And then the next thing was those guys coming up with a nickname for me, which most of you know, because you used it, and that nickname was "Red Bucket." Every time I walk down the hall it was "Hey, Red Bucket! What's up, Red Bucket? Going to class, Red Bucket?" . . . I would like to take this opportunity to ask, what does that even mean??? Like, is it a literal translation where there is a bucket that's red? Or are you saying that there was so much blood that it could have filled a bucket? Because that's stupid—I'd be dead. Okay, Principle Maloney, I'm almost done!

I'm just saying, none of those guys are in honors English with me and while I congratulate them on the usage of two words in a row, everyone knows that insulting nicknames are a single word. And no, Red Bucket is not hyphenated.

The point of my speech is to tell you guys that when we go into high school next year, making fun of me and everyone else stops. They don't do that there. High school is a whole new world, so many things can happen. Becky Rollins might make band by playing the trumpet instead of flute; Gayle Strizinger's mom might show up for a Whopper at her dad's work; and Nittan Mishravi might—well actually, he got early admission at Penn State, so we won't see him any more.

So let's go into Allison Park High School with a clean slate you guys. Let's be new people and be ourselves at the same time. Which, I guess, is just better people. And if not, John Glock got really fat this year and I told my sister who's in tenth grade that his name is Roly Poly John John and that Matt and Chad transferred to our school because they killed a kid.

Go Owls!

Candy Crushed

Kate Mickere

LINDSAY, 14 to 17

LINDSAY *addresses her teacher, Mrs. Peterson, who has just taken her phone away.*

LINDSAY   My name is Lindsay and I am an addict.

I'm addicted to Candy Crush.

I know that's not a particularly glamorous or hard-core addiction . . . and by "glamorous," I mean I couldn't get on a celebrity rehab show for it, but . . . it's still a serious problem!

Being addicted to Candy Crush is super lame, I know. It's basically a game for moms. But just because it isn't a particularly life-threatening addiction doesn't mean I shouldn't be treated with the same amount of respect and tender care that Lindsay Lohan gets every time she hangs out with Oprah.

So, please, can I have my phone back, Mrs. Peterson?

[*Beat.*]

Would you just take drugs away from a druggie and make them stop cold turkey? No! Or, maybe you do, I don't actually know . . . but I think they probably need to be weaned from it. I need to be weaned from it. I'm getting withdrawals and the shakes and I can't concentrate, unless I'm turning pieces of candy into candy bombs.

It's just so pleasing, watching the matching candies as they glide into place. Finally making it to the next level so that weird pigtailed little girl can make it over the bubblegum bridge. It's the only time in my life I've ever actually been encouraged to eat *more* chocolate. You should really try it, Mrs. Peterson.

I wish I could stop. Do you know how much anxiety I get when I'm stuck on a timed level? Or when I can't eat all the chocolate and it totally engulfs my screen? My heart rate quickens . . . I get sweaty and nervous . . . I don't even do that in gym class!

What if I did another kind of punishment? You could give me my phone back and I could write across the board, Bart Simpson style. Or we could go old-school retro and you can smack me across the palms like they do to Kirsten Dunst in *Little Women* when she has too many limes.

[LINDSAY *has a moment of realization.*]

This is the exact same situation! Susan Sarandon takes Kirsten Dunst out of school because her teacher is a barbarian and doesn't want her to keep fruit in her desk. Do you WANT me to be homeschooled, Mrs. Peterson?

[*Beat.*]

No, I've haven't read the book. My mom just makes us watch it every Christmas. And speaking of my mother, do you know how much she pays for my cell phone? She's not busting her butt at work so you can keep my phone in your desk.

I take that back. I'm so sorry.

Do you know what Snapchat is? That's what you should be railing against, not me. Right now, every one is doing very questionable things on their phone while we're having this conversation. Candy Crush is not the enemy.

[*Pause.*]

You'll let me have it back? Oh my god, thank you, Mrs. Peterson!

I just have to write a book report on *Little Women* for you by Monday. I guess I walked myself right into that one, didn't I? But I said I'd do anything . . . and you know what? A book report is easy when you can take breaks to travel over the Cotton Candy Mountain. I'll do it!

One-Sided Conversation

Katie Willert

ALICIA, 15

ALICIA *sits down on a toilet in the bathroom stall. She sits for a beat.*

ALICIA   Beth. I know you're in there. It's okay. I PROMISE. No one saw. [*Beat.*] Okay, some people saw. But you covered it really well, which is awesome! Seriously though, stuff like this happens all the time. It takes a while to get used to the swing of things. I didn't even know how to handle what was going on for, like, the first three months. Just *vroom* [*Gestures over her head.*] over my head. Heh. So . . .

[*No answer. Long beat.*]

Look, you had your period everywhere. And I'm talking EVERYWHERE. It looks like someone went to town with an axe in the cafeteria. It's actually kind of epic. I guess my point is that it's already happened, you can't change it, so you should just hold your head high and walk out of this bathroom with victory. Once we get you a change of pants, that is. But, I mean, you're a woman now! How awesome is that?!? Our bodies can do all of this hard-core stuff and we live through it. My mom told me that once, when she was a teenager, she had such intense PMS that when a guy whistled at her from a pickup truck, she walked right up to the truck and punched the window out! THAT'S power. And there's nothing gross about it, either. I mean, after a while, you just get used to the fact that you are bleeding profusely and yet still going about your day like a warrior. THAT'S strength.

[*Still no answer.*]

One time, in the fifth grade, I thought I had gotten my period because when I turned around after going pee, the toilet water was red. I went to the nurse and she gave me some tampons and pads and stuff and told me how to use them. I put one in and kept it in for a couple of hours. I thought it was time to change it, but when I went to pull it out, I couldn't. It was stuck. Like, way stuck. I went into freak-out mode and my mom didn't know what to do, so she stuck me in a bathtub and I sat there for, no joke, three HOURS until I could finally get it out. My mom found out that the medication I was taking for some teeny poop worms sometimes turns pee red. Who knew? So there. Now you know two super embarrassing stories about me. And the world didn't end, right? We're both still here. So come on out of that stall and we'll finish lunch. I got you cool blue Gatorade because I know blue is your favorite flavor . . .

[*Nothing.*]

Did you fall in? [ALICIA *bends down to look under the stall wall.*] Man! How'd you manage to get your Toms so clean? I mean they were just SOAKED in—Oh. Oh my gosh. You're not Beth, are you? Nope. No, you are definitely not Beth. [*Panicking.*] Everything I said? Before? Yeah, it was a lie. I just wanted to make Beth feel better, so I made up this huge, MAJOR story that would put everything in perspective! It definitely wasn't the truth! Not the truth at all! I mean, I didn't get a tampon stuck in my vagina. What? That's ridiculous! I also didn't have teeny tiny little poop worms, either! My poop is clean! Clean as a whistle! You can guarantee that didn't happen to me, or my name isn't Alicia

Van Shenker. [*Beat.*] You didn't know my name before, did you? [*Beat.*] SAY SOMETHING! What is your problem? HUH? Do you just sit in bathrooms, waiting for people to divulge their deepest secrets? You're a sicko! You know that? You're sick! And I'll be looking out for you, WHITE TOMS! You better watch your back!

[ALICIA *slams her hand on the stall and then storms out.*]

Valedictorian Speech

Jessica Glassberg

JAMIE, 18

JAMIE, *the class valedictorian, wears a cap and gown as she addresses her fellow classmates.*

JAMIE   Good afternoon to my fellow classmates, faculty, and staff. It is an honor to be standing here as your valedictorian.

It seems like only yesterday that we tiptoed through the doors of Kennedy High as nervous ninth graders. Who didn't get lost in the east wing that first week? Or month? Or yesterday?

[*She waits for laughs.*]

We've all grown up since our first homeroom bell. We've made lifelong friends and . . .

[*She stops and thinks. She's going off-book.*]

At least that's what they tell you in movies. That high school is where you meet your best friends for life. Yes, I watch movies. Usually by myself or with my mom and her friend Barb, but I watch them. And I've watched all of you. But I wonder, have you seen me?

Everyone knows me as Jamie Krauss, the mathlete, or Jamie Krauss the Model UN secretary general. Or yes, Jamie Krauss, that girl who fell off the stage during her jazz band alto sax solo.

You can stop e-mailing me the video. I've seen it. It was on the KCBT News. We've all seen it. But like I said, have you really seen me?

Well, I saw everything. I saw you laughing at me at the tenth-grade dance-a-thon when I did the running man for seventy-three minutes straight. I pulled my groin. My whole groin. Really badly. That's why I was walking weird for a month. Not because I did it with a donkey!

I saw some of you shoplift the new Paradise Pink lip glow lip gloss when it came out. Did any of you think to share some with me? I don't have herpes. I've never kissed anyone!

And yes, I saw you all smoke pot in the field behind the deli. Would it have been so hard to ask me if I wanted to get high? Maybe the smartest girl in school wouldn't pass on grass?

And when I say, "I saw it all," I literally mean, I saw it all. I took pictures of everything. My parents got me this crazy data plan, but I don't have anyone to take selfies with or text . . .

So, if you don't want these pot pics going viral, or you don't want your parents to know you were one of the girls giving out handies in chem lab during sixth period, I suggest you start inviting me to your parties so I can have a summer to remember, or black out from, before I head for the Ivy Leagues.

Thanks in advance for the memories. Go Hawks!

Bad Day

Leah Mann

JESSIE, 17

JESSIE, *a sporty, capable, wry high school junior stares at a flat tire on the back of her car while her boyfriend stands uselessly next to her.*

JESSIE   Great, the tire is flat. How does that even happen? Did I drive over a nail or something? This sucks. I guess it's good that the car isn't broken. A flat tire doesn't count as broken, does it? This is all pretty new to me.

[*Beat.*]

I don't suppose *you* can fix it?

[*Beat.*]

Never? Your dad didn't show you or anything? . . . Right, sorry, I didn't mean to subscribe to stereotypical gender roles. If I can't change a tire, there's no reason you should be able to. Though really, we should BOTH be able to do this. It's not a guy/girl thing; it should be a driver thing, like part of the test to get your license.

[*Beat.*]

We're smart, right? Stupider people than us must have changed tires before—I'm sure we can figure it out. We just need to jack up the car, and get the iron thingy. Is there a car jack?

[*Beat.*]

Right, it's my car—why would you know? Technically it's my dad's car, but your point stands. Um, the trunk, the trunk, the trunk . . . Popping the trunk . . .

[*She's searching through the trunk.*]

Jesus, I don't think my dad has ever cleaned this out. Check out all this shit—camping gear, work papers, softball stuff, dirty towels . . . we haven't gone to the beach in two years . . . yikes. Is this a jack? No, that's a hammer. Will a hammer be helpful? Probably not.

[*Beat.*]

I found it! Tire iron, that's what it's called . . . But no jack. Crap.

[*Beat.*]

Did you call your brother? I think we're going to have to wait for help. . . . Unless you can lift up the car while I use the tire iron . . . ? You're sure there's no adrenaline rushing through your veins in this time of danger and need giving you superhuman strength? 'Cause that'd be really handy—

[*Beat.*]

I'm not trying to emasculate you. I was just asking. It WOULD be handy, you have to admit.

[*He starts to walk away from her. She yells after him in disbelief.*]

Come back. I was joking! If I liked you for your physical prowess, I wouldn't like you. I like you for your mental prowess and emotional maturity. Remember your emotional maturity?!

[*Beat.*]

You can't seriously be leaving me here on the side of the road in the middle of the night with a flat tire?

[*Beat.*]

I'm not calling my parents, because it's three a.m. and I'm supposed to be at Risa's house. You could call your parents because they don't care what you do and they love me and want us to stay together forever so I can be a positive influence and make beautiful babies with you after graduating from a reputable university and establishing my career.

[*Beat.*]

Don't get mad. It's the truth and you know it. You told me so yourself, and so did your mom. Come on, give your bro a call. We can snuggle up in the backseat while we wait. It'll be creepy and romantic like in a horror movie . . . only without the serial killer or werewolf. Unless it's a sexy werewolf who saves us from a serial killer. Or a sexy serial killer who slays a wolf . . . no, that one doesn't work as well. I take it back.

[*Beat.*]

I bet my dad even has some beer hidden in all this mess. Which is very irresponsible of him, but since we won't be driving anywhere we might as well indulge. Right? We can salvage this day.

[*She starts looking through the trunk again.*]

Yes, it was a rough one. You failed biology and I lost the swim meet to Carrie Newsom of all people, and I found out my parents are getting divorced and your sister's chemo isn't going well, plus the whole food poisoning thing at the party—boy am I glad I don't eat shrimp—I mean, I guess I'd be grumpy too if I'd spent forty minutes shitting in a gas station bathroom like you—but

we're here now. It's a clear night, the stars are sparkling, we
have . . .

[*Beat.*]

. . . gin! Okey-dokey Dad, gin, sure . . .

[*She opens her arms as he heads back towards her.*]

There he is, there's that smile. Come save the night with me. Call
your brother and while we wait, we'll fog up the windows so
much we can't even see all those stars.

[*Beat.*]

Your phone is dead?

[*Beat.*]

It was just working—

[*She hears something.*]

Did you hear that? I swear I hear footsteps . . . Is it getting cloudy
out all of the sudden? What's your brother's number? I'll call
him—

[*She turns away while rummaging to find her phone.*]

My phone should still be alive . . .

[*It's quiet. Too quiet. She looks up nervously.*]

Alex?

[*Where did he go?*]

ALEX!?! . . .

[*She hears another noise, an awful one.*]

Is that gurgling your stomach? From the shrimp? . . . Alex?

[*Yelps.*]

Oh, um … Hi there, stranger who isn't Alex.

[*Beat.*]

You haven't seen my boyfriend? Five ten, brown hair, nice eyes . . . ?

[*Beat.*]

Not much of a talker, are you?

[*Beat.*]

Isn't it a beautiful night, with the moon reflecting off that large bloody blade in your hand? . . . I don't suppose you have a car jack, too?

[*Beat.*]

Just the machete . . . Any chance you're a sexy serial killer with personal code of honor?

[*Beat.*]

Just a regular old psychopath. Okay, this really has been a bad day.

Golf

Alessandra Rizzotti

STEPHANIE, 13

STEPHANIE *sits in band class. She seems to need to go to the bathroom, but she's clearly holding it in. She talks to a band mate, Lily.*

STEPHANIE   Is that an F-sharp? I can't tell these days. My eyes are getting a little messed up. The doctor says I'm growing or something so I need to eat carrots. No, I don't need to go to the bathroom. I just have restless leg syndrome. I'm not going to explain it to you again, Lily. There's no point if you don't know how it feels.

Gosh, when is Mr. Barry coming back? Is he smoking weed in the bathroom again or something? I'm itching to march already. I gotta get this energy out. My bassoon is waiting. Pretty cool that I'm the only one that plays this thing, by the way, isn't it? I wasn't going to say you made a bad choice with the French horn, but come onnnn.

[*There's an awkward pause.* STEPHANIE *has clearly offended Lily.*]

Hey Lily, have you ever golfed? It's become my new favorite hobby. Basically, I'm probably going pro at Claremont when I get in. I mean, I don't know if I'm in yet, but I'm pretty sure of my abilities and I just have a feeling that God is like, you're getting in, girl. That is, if he doesn't find out about, you know, me.

[STEPHANIE *lowers her eyes and whispers at Lily.*]

Lily, come on, you've known I've had a crush on Sarah for like, ever. I just never tell anyone because I don't want it to be blasted in our school newsletter that I deserve love and respect on LGBT Pride Day because duh, everyone deserves love and respect every day. I'm not the LGBT mascot of this place. Although, wouldn't it be funny if in band we had a rainbow as a mascot and a leprechaun chasing it during halftime? Ha-ha. So good.

Oh, there's Mr. Barry. Finally. Yup. Smells like weed. I swear, if we weren't in art school with all the Waldorf kids from middle school, I'd report him. But, whatevs, that's what we get for having hippie parents. I swear golf saves me from this bullshit. You should try it some time.

Gothic Love

Daisy Faith

SALEM, 14

SALEM, *a Wiccan, goth girl, who is a super sourpuss and somewhat dark and scary, sits cross-legged in a meditative pose with candles, wand in hand, and a plate of snickerdoodle cookies on the floor in her goth bedroom. She is holding a one-woman séance, trying to connect with her dead grandma. Later, she starts making a love spell with her cauldron and spell book.*

SALEM   [*Eyes closed, chanting.*] Olm, olm. Our beloved Granny Judith Mavis Sampsonite, we bring you gifts from life into death. Commune with us, Granny Judith, and among us. Olm . . .

[*No response from the spirit world. A black cat, Raven, approaches. SALEM pets the cat.*]

Raven, I guess Granny Judith doesn't find the aroma of her favorite snickerdoodles pleasing *or* all pumpkin-vanilla candles! She must not have been hungry or lacking mood lighting when she died.

[*Suddenly SALEM hears a voice calling her.*]

[*Demon-possessed voice.*] What, Mom?!

[*Back to normal voice.*] Raven, where's your sister, Pentagram? Come here, Pentagram—fine don't!! I'll read your palm later. I guess we'll talk to Granny another time. Back to Seamus

Devereaux, the creator and president of the Ninth Grade Wicca Club and the cutest warlock I know. Let's see what the love spell says.

[SALEM *opens a huge spell book and situates the caldron.*] Eye of newt! Well, we don't have that! We'll just have to use baking soda instead . . . dolls, photographs, rue, clover . . . [*Glancing over at cats, evilly.*] We already got the cat whiskers. Stop looking at me like that, Pentagram—it's all in the name of love! So now we just stir and sing . . . "Love, love, come around, make these two into one, love, love come around now . . . Love potion number 9!!!"

[*Picks up her wand and smacks caldron.*]

Bam! It even smells like love! Now all we have to do is bind Seamus and gag him after the Wicca meeting and douse him. He won't remember a thing. Alchemy rocks!

[*Demon voice.*] In a minute, Mom!

[*Back to normal voice.*] Raven, I don't know why I have to have dinner with Mom tonight. She's never here anyway. Two workaholics really shouldn't be allowed to reproduce. It's amazing that I've made it to fourteen if you think about it, especially since Mom and Dad are never around to thwart my botched spells and schemes. I mean they still haven't noticed that when I was twelve I changed my name from Samantha to Salem Sampsonite.

[*Angered, she's heard this joke one too many times.*] No, not like the luggage, Pentagram—the p is silent! Fact! I smell frozen lasagna for dinner. Gross muggle food.

[SALEM *stands up.*]

[*Demon voice.*] Coming, Mom!!

Jenny and the Missing Flip-Flops

Chrissy Swinko

JENNY, 17 to 18

At the front desk of her local police station, JENNY *is reporting a crime.*

JENNY   Can someone please help me? I need to report a crime.

My name is Jennifer MacArthur but everyone calls me Jenny Mac.

Actually, I also called earlier to report it. But I wanted to come in to the station to be sure you had all the details. And to check on the status of the case since 10:00 a.m. That detective said he would get back to me, but I haven't heard anything and it's already 4:00 p.m.!

And tomorrow we're decorating for prom and then this weekend is the prom so I need to get this taken care of as soon as possible!

Okay, I'll tell you again. So, I'm at the nail place sitting in the massage chair, feet soaking, reading a mag, and this woman comes in and there's just something off about her, ya know? Like, my gut—which I trust—is telling me, she is weird.

She asks all kinds of questions about how much it costs to get a mani-pedi and finally she sits down. And then, she left right away when her nails were done. Meanwhile, I'm waiting patiently for mine to dry because *you have to*.

Okay. So finally I'm ready to go. I look down, and my flip-flops are gone. GONE! We all looked everywhere and no flip-flops.

That woman totally stole them!!

And I got them on vacation last July and they were *really* cute. And I was gonna wear them for After Prom! And she was not a size 6 so I don't even know why she took them!

Yes, I *know* it was her! There was no one else there. So what are you going to do about it? My flip-flops are being paraded around town and this is *supposed* to be the best weekend of my life!

Yeah, actually, driving around looking for someone wearing blue and white plaid flip-flops *does* sound like something you could do. That woman is a thief. I don't even want them anymore if they've been on some gross feet. I just want her to get caught because stealing flip-flops is so wrong.

Just so you know, I was head of the sponsorship committee and basically got everything donated for Prom. So I feel like if I can do that, you should be able to find my stolen flip-flops.

Fill out a form and wait?! I already talked to that detective and he filled out the form! This place is a joke. You know if you were still in school, this entire police force would be getting D minuses.

I don't even have time for this. Now I have to go find new flip-flops that match my dress, because Prom Queens have matching flip-flops. And I will not let this thief slow me down.

I have the perfect date and the perfect dress and I *will* have a perfect prom.

What? Fine, if that's all you can do then, yes. I would like a copy of the report for my insurance purposes.

Thank you *so much*! I expect to hear from you soon.

And if I don't, I will be back. With my crown.

Teen Witch

Leah Mann

PRUDENCE, 17 to 18

PRUDENCE *is in the American Colonies. She stands alone on a wooden scaffold, a noose around her neck.*

PRUDENCE   I will not bequeath any forgiveness or cries of regret and repentance upon you undeserving louts. 'Tis bullocks that I stand here before you and no, Reverend, I will NOT mind my tongue, for what does it matter now?

Ye have tried me unjustly and found me guilty of supernatural sins. I say YOU are the sinners.

[*Beat.*]

Did the Widow Haverford come down with scarlet fever mere days after disciplining me for uncouth behavior? Aye, she did. Is it possible that her sickness and death were brought on by a vile curse at my hands in retribution for beating me when I merely shewed her young Zachariah my ankles? If he then lay awake at night with unholy thoughts, 'tis that my fault? Should not the Widow lay some responsibility at her son's hand? His right hand, being the primary offender. And should SHE not have suffered for beating me so harshly, a beating she delivered to me because she is my elder, and permitted to such violence only due to her age? Do not the young have rights?

Speaking of the young, I see many of my young brethren watching me with glee and neither the horror nor sympathy one wouldst hope charitable hearts would give. Is it my actions that hath turned my sisters against me?

[*Beat.*]

If Millicent wanted to keep her hair, she should not have pulled mine so viciously.

Had Temperance not humiliated me during Bible study, might she still have the power of speech today? Certainly she would— but without it she must think before communicating and will not be so quick to be unkind.

Those smarter than me should not mock me for my natural deficiency. A sharp wit is not made to cut those of us with duller minds. Am I slower than some of the other girls? Yes. We all have gifts and weaknesses.

[*Beat.*]

My gift is magic and I use it to teach those who have more natural advantages or inherited wealth humility.

Had Charity lived up to her name and shared her candied apples with me when I was most hungry and experiencing a visit from the moon mother and desperate to eat anything, particularly sweets, mayhap she would have never gotten food poisoning, and mayhap her father's orchards would still be fruitful, and mayhap her baby brother born only two arms.

[*Beat.*]

Yes, I am a witch.

[*Beat.*]

Since my gift is not of speech and I cannot convince thee to free me, and my gift is not of strength so I mayn't break my bonds, nor can I outwit the hangman nor seduce you with any beauty, nor, sadly, does my craft extend to flight or control of the elements—it seems my time has come.

Before you drop me, let me leave you with one final curse . . .

. . . Bear with me a moment, these things do not spew from my lips fully formed . . .

Do NOT touch that lever, hangman . . . give me one moment to formulate the proper words . . .

[*Long beat.*]

Damned. I should have prepared something ahead of time. I don't suppose thou wilst give me half an hour or so? I do want it to be a most horrifying curse that will keep you and your descendants suffering for the ages.

[*Beat.*]

Nay? Once again, you have all proved most uncharitable.

Why-Me-Me?

Liz Kenny

CHELSEA WALKER, 13 to 16

CHELSEA WALKER *is at a gorgeous beach resort in Hawaii. She is lying on the beach under a giant umbrella as the crystal waves crash against the ocean shore.*

CHELSEA   This sucks.

[*Beat.*]

I know we're in Hawaii and everything, but this vacation SUCKS.

[*Beat.*]

I will use the *S* word. And that's not the worst one, Mom. Yeah, I know the other *S* word.

[*Beat.*]

No. I don't want you to wash my mouth out with soap.

Okay. Fine. This vacation . . . is the worst trip ever and I don't know why you ruined my life by taking me to Hawaii.

I'm fifteen and I'm stuck on this sunny, hot island with my nine-year-old-doofus brother and a four-year-old crybaby sister. And I have to share a bed with Grandma.

[*Imitates Grandma.*]

Ooh Chelsea, it's 8:00 p.m. Let's turn the lights out and go to sleep.
Ooh Chelsea, be a dear and put my teeth in a glass by the sink?
Ooh Chelsea, help Gammy put her swimsuit on.

[*Shiver, then back to normal.*]

It should be illegal to wear a swimsuit when you're over fifty.
I'm gonna run for Congress and make it a law. The Anti-Senior
Swimmers Act.

[*Beat.*]

Yeah. I guess it was kinda cool to ride a bike down a volcano. But
we had to get up at like three in the morning to like see the
sunrise at the top of the volcano. I was having cool dreams and
stuff when Dad woke me up.

[*Beat.*]

I was dreaming about winning a volleyball tournament, okay. I
can't even practice my spikes in Hawaii, because none of you
knows how to set the ball.

[*Beat.*]

Ugh. You don't know anything. It's a move in volleyball.

[*Beat.*]

I know we swam with dolphins. They're like all over the ocean.
It's like the squirrel of the ocean. Who cares?

[*Beat.*]

But you better not tell anyone that my first kiss was a dolphin. I
didn't kiss him back!

[*Beat.*]

[*Irritated moan.*]

We were stuck on that boat for three hours and the whales didn't even have cool names. I mean Kiki and Tok-Tok? The only cool part was Dad barfing over the back the back of the boat.

[*Beat.*]

Yeah, that is cool. The video got a ton of likes on Insta.

[*Beat.*]

No. None of my friends have been to Hawaii.

[*Beat.*]

Yeah. I'm really lucky. God.

[*Beat.*]

No, Mom. I don't want a picture with the parrots.

[*Raises her right arm and watches a parrot crawl from her elbow to her shoulder.*]

What if they poop on me?

[*Raises her left arm and watches a parrot crawl from her elbow to her shoulder.*]

These parrots look hungry, Mom.

[*Looks on top of her head while someone places a parrot on her head.*]

Say "Waikiki"? More like Why-Me-Me?

Hall Pass

Angi Lenhart

LILLY, 17

LILLY, *nervous and rambling, is sitting outside 5th-period English class at the hall monitor table, speaking to Nathan.*

LILLY Hey, Nathan, about Friday night . . . [*Nervous laughter.*] That was just crazy. I mean it was so funny, I mean, why are cops even patrolling country roads by your house, anyway? It was so weird.

Ya know, I totally forgot you even lived on, what was it, County Rd. P? Or was it 6a—I don't even remember—that was just . . . [*Shakes her head.*] I didn't even realize they could pick you up for curfew . . . that's so stupid. I mean, I'm an adult. Well, not legally, but . . . ya know, emotionally. And physically. And, I mean . . . ya know . . . We're not babies; we don't need babysitters.

But Officer Bruback was super cool about it . . . I mean, obviously, I'm in volleyball with his daughter, so he couldn't be like a total jerk, but . . . there's only so much he could do. I still have to go in front of the judge, but, only in his office . . . not like, the courtroom; no jury of my peers!

And thank you for coming out to check on me and Maya. That was really sweet! I mean, it was nice. It was so late that . . . I was really surprised you were still awake. You must be a night person. I am too. I'm a total night owl.

Anyway, it was just . . . we were just out driving. I mean, we were talking and driving, and just listening to music, and like, out for a drive, ya know? The football game was over, everybody was going in different directions, and Maya's mom works third shift, so we had the whole night to do whatever we wanted, and . . . I just had no idea about the time. And I didn't realize city curfew was eleven! And I did NOT know we were right by your house. Like, right there. In front. [*Shakes head.*] So weird.

And, listen, Nathan . . . I know Ruben told you that I wanted you to ask me to Homecoming and that's NOT what I said. Ruben was talking about Homecoming, and I was like, "Well, who would you want to take?"
And he was like, "Alyssa or Danielle."
And I was like, "Well, you have to pick one! Just ONE."
And he was like, "Fine, Danielle!"
And I was like, "Okay. Why didn't you just say that?"
And he was like, "I dunno . . . you asked me outta the blue and I was just brainstorming!" And he's like, "Who would YOU take?"
And I was like, "Well, I dunno. I dunno, I mean, maybe Nathan or . . ."
And he was like, "No 'or'! You have to pick ONE person."
And I was like, "Fine! Nathan."

Because I thought, like, who would be cool to go with? Who would be a cool person?

And please don't tell Ruben I told you about Danielle. 'Cause I'm pretty sure that conversation was strictly confidential.

So, see? We were just, like . . . brainstorming. It was like, a spur-of-the-moment question, and we gave, like, totally random . . . answers. Ya know, like, who would be fun to go with?

I mean . . . if you had to pick. And . . . I think you'd be fun to go with.

[*Beat.*]

You're welcome.

Anyway, I'm not even sure if I can go to Homecoming—my ankle's still sprained from the mole holes in your yard! [*Catches herself.*] I mean, unless you want to go with me . . . then I'm sure it would be fine by then. I could wear flats!

[*Catches herself again, quickly.*] Ya know what . . . here's your hall pass. And Mr. Hamlin said he'd like you back AS SOON as possible.

The Failure of the 4.0

Ryane Nicole Granados

CADENCE, 17

CADENCE *and Aubrey are in a study room of the library at their local high school.* CADENCE *is a 17-year-old high school senior and her best friend, Aubrey, is a fellow senior, too. They are both self-proclaimed "nerds," poised to embark on a senior ditch day to remember.*

CADENCE   So get this, Aubrey. It turns out my lame-ass stepbrother was right. He was right all along and now I'm screwed. I have totally set myself up for a monumental fail and it's all because of my obsession with good grades. I didn't even need my mom to post my As on the fridge. I posted them up myself and made copies so I could display them in my room for all who entered to see. I spent years of my life fixating over every single assignment, all to get to this moment and discover none of it even matters. Now I have to write an essay to get into college and the one school I really want to go to is asking me to describe the things that make me who I am "outside of the classroom." Are they kidding me? Outside of the damn classroom! Wasn't the whole point to focus on the inside of the classroom?

I remember my stupid stepbrother would say: "You've got it all wrong kid. You think these As mean something, but in reality they just mean there is nowhere else for you to go. See me. I keep 'em guessing with C minuses. Down is good, because you have room to rise up. When I graduate, your mom and my dad will be filled with such shock and happiness, I'll be able to get whatever I want from 'em. But when you graduate, it will have this anticlimatic, 'just another Saturday' effect. Who cares, they'll think. Plans will be made for your room months before you head off to college. Next week you should put a C minus on the fridge, baby sis."

And to make matters worse, he would offer his philosophies with a mouth full of Lucky Charms or Cinnamon Toast Crunch served in a mixing bowl and eaten with a soup ladle so that he didn't have to return for seconds. Why would I listen to someone eating cereal out of a mixing bowl?

It's the purest definition of irony, and my GPA is the punch line to a cruel joke. Truth is, no one actually cares about my 4.0, and now I have only a few months to get a freakin' life that has nothing to do with school. We're at a critical point, Aubrey—a point of no return. It's do-or-die time, and "Mission: Get a Life" begins with senior ditch day!

I'll do some research. No wait! That's too academic! Instead, I'll make a list. A bucket list. A list of all the things I plan to do before I lay to rest my pointless high school career.

Number One: I'm going to kiss Julian! And not just a summer camp peck, but a real tongue-on-tongue gold-medal-worthy kiss. It'll be so passionate that I'll feel it in the back of my knees, and right at the moment of almost collapsing he'll pull me even closer; he'll kiss me even harder.

Number Two: We must pull an all-nighter. Not an all-nighter because we're up late studying, but an all-nighter because the night will be too epic to waste sleeping. We'll try food we've never had before—like real sushi. No more imitation California Roll pretend sushi, but the sushi college co-eds probably eat.

Then we'll go to a concert or a nightclub or both. Fake ID (Check), Dancing Shoes (Check), and before the night is over we'll crowd surf in the air on the arms of sweaty, shouting strangers carrying us to a new level of awesomeness.

And finally, Number Three: To wash off the stench of smoke, and sweat, and other people's perfume, we'll end the night to rival all nights by skinny-dipping! We'll dive into the Pacific butt-ass naked! Do you hear me? Naked! Screaming at the top of our lungs. Calling out to the moon and stars. Yes, it'll be cold! Yes, it'll be crazy. Cold, Crazy, Carefree, You and Me.

Are you in, Aubrey? I can't do this without you. It's time to close these worthless books, so we can look into ourselves and find out exactly what we're really made of! If nothing else, at least I'll have something to write this college essay about. My title will be, "I Still Can't Believe My Stepbrother Was Actually Right!"

Judgment Day

Leah Mann

DANICA, 16 to 18

DANICA *is a high school cheerleading captain and popular kid queen bee.* DANICA *stands sweating in a ring of fire and brimstone.*

DANICA   Oh my god, where the hell am I? Is this real? It's so freakin' hot in here.

[*Beat.*]

Are you a demon?!!

[*Beat.*]

An imp? Is that supposed to be better? I don't think that's better, you're still ugly and . . . Ow! Don't poke me with that.

[*Beat.*]

Oh. My. God . . .

[*Beat.*]

I'm in hell. That's where the hell I am. Meta.

[*Beat.*]

Is this about that time I tried to send Julia back to the hospital? Because that was like, three years ago, and I'm a much better big sister now. I give her free haircuts and expose her to all sorts of new things. She sticks to me like a little leech—she must love me.

[*Beat.*]

Or is this about taking that picture of Serena while she was going to the bathroom, and texting it to like, the whole school? Because I got grounded and had my phone taken away for a month for doing that, so I think I already paid the price for that one. And Serena isn't mad at me anymore—I mean, it was super funny— which she totally gets and we don't hold grudges.

[*Beat.*]

. . . Or is this because I sabotaged Devin's tryout for cheerleading? I'm not going to apologize for that. He got on the team anyways because "diversity," and everyone thinks it's so cool for a boy to be a cheerleader even though he has NO rhythm. I'm all for equal opportunity and stuff, but part of being equal is that if you suck, you should have to deal with the same rejection as everyone else, and Devin sucks. It worked out for him because everyone pitied him so much he got super popular and he didn't have to walk for like, six weeks because of his cast. He never admitted it, but I know he loved the attention and he's lazy, so getting pushed around in a wheelchair is his secret fantasy—which I made come true for him.

He thanked me, no joke. Everyone was crowded around signing his cast and I was like, "You should be glad I saved you the humiliation of performing with a squad way out of your league." And he was like, "Yeah, thanks so much for breaking my leg. You're the best."

[*Beat.*]

Maybe he was being sarcastic—it's hard for me to tell sometimes, because I'm not very good at reading people and he uses words that like, no one our age ever uses . . . but I'm pretty sure he meant it.

[*Beat.*]

Whoa. Is THAT Satan?

[*Beat.*]

He's cute. Most guys can't pull off the soul patch, but he owns it. Can you introduce me? Maybe he can help me out with this silly little mix-up. You're obviously too low on the totem pole. I mean, who were you before you died? Like one of those angry boys who hated girls who wouldn't go out with him because he was "a nice guy" but never bothered to actually, like, groom themselves or listen to what a girl was really saying? I've rejected so many guys like that. Just because you're a nerd doesn't mean you're nice.

[*Beat.*]

Is that why I'm here? Revenge? Are you Franklin from middle school? Because I know I pretended to like you back and then made posters of all those love poems you wrote me and put them around the school after publicly humiliating you at the seventh grade Winter Formal, but that was ages ago and you still looked cool for showing up at the dance with me. Plus you should stand behind your work—if those poems were so embarrassing, why would you send them to me in the first place?

[*Beat.*]

I realize that all SOUNDS like I'm mean or whatever, but I'm not. I did three weeks of community service last summer and it was awful, but I did it without complaining which was insanely saintly of me. Yeah, I HAD to for school but still, I totally threw myself into it and was soo nice to the old people even though they smelled like the hospital, which makes me want to puke. Honestly, the sulfur and rotting-egg smell here is better.

So can I like go home now? Or at least to purgatory or something? We can agree it's pretty obvious I do NOT belong here.

I mean, what the hell?!

Abduct Me, Already!

Andra Whipple

LILY, 11 to 13

LILY *is in middle school. She is talking to the school principal, Principal Withers.*

LILY   What's my goal in life? Well, I'm really trying to get abducted by aliens. It would make the seventh grade so much more interesting. I mean, don't get me wrong, I love PE class, and I would hate it if getting abducted interfered with going to see my brother's violin concert, because I sorta promised I would be there. I have a lot going on, but I'd be willing to put my schedule on hold for an opportunity this important. A girl's gotta have priorities. And getting abducted is definitely my number one, because sometimes I just feel like life, and the world around me, is so much bigger than Centerville, Ohio. The biggest thing that has happened this month was when the cafeteria switched from fries to tater tots. Which of course was a definite win, but still not enough to keep me earth-bound. I've been to Claire's at the mall every single day this week, and I just don't know how many more bracelets I can buy. I only have two wrists! I've got like twenty bracelets on right now and they keep jangling together, which is basically making my layup shot impossible, and they give me a rash anyways. The other day I got excited because somebody asked me to go to Costco, and I knew I would get minicheesecake samples. That's the kind of thing a kid in this town gets excited about. Minicheesecake. Minicheesecake is great, but it shouldn't be the most exciting thing you do all year. Life is about exploring more than just chocolate chip swirl versus original. I have a lot to see. And the aliens are going to help me see it.

And yes, when I'm eighteen I could go to college, and travel the world with my trusty sidekick, and become a famous basketball player. I could learn the trumpet and eat dinner at the White House with president Rihanna and have a brief affair with an overdramatic opera singer named Paolo. I could eat Costco minicheesecakes by the sea, and share them with my whale friends while Paolo sings "Con te partiro" accompanied by a steel-drum orchestra. I could learn how to pilot an airplane, and make a Manhattan, and be a sophisticated woman of the world who owns multiple shades of lipstick. I could pile all of my belongings into an RV and drive across Bhutan befriending the locals. I could get married to a circus clown and quickly realize that I'm allergic to elephants and our relationship is doomed. The divorce would be tragic, but still kind of funny in that weird way that clowns are. I could invent my own line of cashmere socks embroidered with funny dogs and sell them exclusively to celebrities. I could ride a horse across the Egyptian desert and go swimming in the depths of the Arctic accompanied by penguins. Adulthood is full of opportunities, and I intend to exploit them all in due time. But for the time being I am twelve.

And at twelve, what can I do now? Nothing! I am bored! So I feel like the extraction of a few organs is definitely worth a few more years of adventure, and a few less years of bumming around the CVS. It's not that there's nothing to do here, but I've already stolen a shopping cart, tipped a cow, and kissed a boy, so I think I've pretty much seen what southern Ohio has to offer. I've extracted all of it's potential, and I'm only twelve. How do you expect me to give this place six more years of my life? It has nothing to offer me.

And sure, my parents would be devastated if I was beamed up to a UFO never to return again, but I think, in the end, when I'm the first human to colonize Neptune, they'll be pretty glad about it. Who wouldn't be proud to have their daughter brokering alien peace treaties? That is literally the coolest legacy I can think of for a parent. And since I'll have gained their trust and be fluent in their language, I'll be their chief communicator within the human race. I'll sign the first official treaty of alien-human cooperation, and include important provisions to assure that the Earth isn't overrun by Doctor Who's worst nightmares. I'll solve the problem of orphans by orchestrating alien-human adoptions. I'll foster alien-human harmony and create a world where all are welcome. I have big dreams, and it's time to take them skyward bound. Life isn't about in standing in one place—it's about making crop circles in my grandpa's cornfield to signal to the invaders that I'm friend, not foe. It's about boning up on my scientific knowledge so that I can explain to my new friends why I need oxygen, and they'd better get me some soon. It's about locking myself in the freezer at my uncle's restaurant so that I can better withstand the extreme temperature shifts of alien planets. It's about carefully studying linguistics to be able to interpret brand-new languages I could have never even imagined before.

So, no, Principal Withers, I'm not at all concerned about my D minus in English class. It is the least of my worries. Aliens probably don't even speak English, so what's the point? I have much, much bigger horizons on my mind. English just isn't a priority when you have goals as definite as mine. I'm a dreamer, Principal Withers, and I dream about the open sky. I know the aliens are coming for me. All I have to do is prepare, and then I'm off. As Shakespeare says, the sky is my oyster. See? I know stuff about English after all.

Contributors

ALISHA GADDIS is a Latin Grammy and Emmy Award–winning performer and actress, humorist, writer, and producer based in Los Angeles. She is a graduate of New York University's Tisch School of the Arts and the University of Sydney, Australia.

Alisha's first book, *Women's Comedic Monologues That Are Actually Funny*, was published by Hal Leonard/Applause Books in 2014. Subsequently, she signed on with Hal Leonard to release five more books in this series, which includes the book you are currently holding in your hands. Her columns have appeared in College Candy, Comediva, *GOOD* magazine, and Thought Catalog. Alisha is the founder and head writer of Say Something Funny . . . B*tch!— the nationally acclaimed all-female online magazine. The highly irreverent Messenger Card line that she cofounded and writes for is sold in boutiques nationally.

Alisha currently stars in the TV show she cocreated and executive-produced, *Lishy Lou and Lucky Too*, as part of the Emmy Award–winning children's series *The Friday Zone* on PBS/PBS KIDS.

Alongside her husband, Lucky Diaz, she is the cofounder and performer for Latin Grammy Award–winning Lucky Diaz and the Family Jam Band. Their children's music has topped the charts at Sirius XM and is *People* magazine's No. 1 album of the year—playing Los Angeles Festival of Books, Target Stage, the Smithsonian, the Getty Museum, Madison Square Park, Legoland, New York City's Symphony Space, and more. Their song "Falling" has been used in Coca-Cola's summer national ad campaign.

As a stand-up comic and improviser, Alisha has headlined the nation at the World Famous Comedy Store and the New York Comedy Club, and has been named one of the funniest upcoming female comics by *Entertainment Weekly*. As a performer, she has appeared on Broadway; has performed at the Sydney Opera House, Second City Hollywood, Improv Olympic West, Upright Citizens Brigade, and the Comedy Central Stage; and has toured with her acclaimed solo shows *Step-Parenting: The Last Four Letter Word* and *The Search for Something Grand*. She has also appeared on MTV, CBS, CNN, Univision, NBC, and A&E, and has voiced many national campaigns. Alisha is a proud SAG-AFTRA, NARAS, LARAS, and AEA member.

She loves her husband the most.

www.alishagaddis.com

TIFFANY E. BABB is a Los Angeles–based writer and book hoarder. She is currently finishing up her Comparative Literature degree at the University of Southern California and slaving away on her thesis about the duality of Marvel Comics' Loki. Babb enjoys reading novels, poetry, and comics. Some of her favorite writers include John le Carré, W. H. Auden, Emily Dickinson, and Greg Rucka. When she isn't reading or writing, Babb likes to attend comic book conventions, eat brunch, and think about impending doom (usually at separate times). You can find some of her comics at *tiffanyebabb.com*.

BRAXTON BROOKS is an Los Angeles–based actress, comedienne, and writer. Originally from Washington, DC, Braxton began her career as a dancer and studied at both the Alvin Ailey American Dance Theater and the Dance Theatre of Harlem schools. She attended Harvard University and graduated magna cum laude with a degree in performance studies. Academia helped her realize she prefers producing artistic work to analyzing it. With Meisner training from William Esper Studios and Improv training from Second City Hollywood, Braxton has appeared on and off-Broadway and in several regional stage productions as well as national ad campaigns for VH1 and USA. For more information or career updates from Braxton, check out *BraxtonBrooks.com* or follow Braxton on Twitter *@tweetbraxtonb*.

CARLA CACKOWSKI is an actress and playwright living in Los Angeles. Carla toured the world performing comedy (on a boat!) with comedy troupe The Second City. She currently teaches improvisation at The Second City in Hollywood. Carla has written and performed five comedic solo shows that have played in Los Angeles, New York City, San Diego, Dallas, and Austin. She's a member of The Solo Collective, a theater company in residence at VS. Theatre Company in Los Angeles. Several of her monologues were published in *Women's Comedic Monologues That Are Actually Funny* (Applause Books, 2014). She is a member of SAG-AFTRA and, as a voice-over artist, has been featured on television shows such as *iCarly*, *Pretty Little Liars*, and *Cougar Town*. Carla was a writer on *Lishy Lou and Lucky Too*, an adorably hilarious children's show that aired on PBS KIDS. Special thanks to Alisha Gaddis for being a superhero by inspiring us all to do more than we thought we could. Find her online at *www.carlacackowski.com*.

KAYLA CAGAN is a writer and dramaturg living in Los Angeles with her husband and their dog, Banjo. Kayla is a member of the Dramatists Guild and Literary Managers and Dramaturgs of the Americas. Her plays *Blue in the Face*, *Halasana*, and *Shot Americans* are published by Smith and Kraus. Her play *Roller Coaster* is published in *Many Mountains Moving* literary journal. Her monologue "Dog People" is featured in the anthology *One on One: Playing with a Purpose: Monologues for Kids Ages 7–15* (Applause Books, 2013).

Her ten-minute play *Band Geeks* was published in *25 10-Minute Plays for Teens* (Applause Books, 2014). Her monologues "Margo Maine Doesn't Live Here Anymore," "Cannonball," and "The Peanut Allergy," as well as her ten-minute play *Fight of Fright*, will be published in Applause anthologies in late 2015. She's also written two comic books. Tweet and talk theater, writing, ice cream, and dogs with her *@KaylaCagan*.

LAUREN CANDIA is the cocreator and cohost of the Shades & Shadows Reading Series, Los Angeles's creepiest ongoing literary happening. It's literature, but with monsters! When not cooking up ways to make Los Angeles just a little more frightening, Lauren works at a library where she spends a great deal of time trying to convince people they should love all the same books she loves. She writes weird stories with a tiny dog and an extremely understanding fiancé somewhere nearby. Her writing can be found in the *East Jasmine Review* and the *Los Angeles Times*. She will be your BFF on Facebook and Twitter (*@ParanormaLauren*). All you have to do is ask.

SAMANTHA CARDONA is an actress and writer from Northern California. She graduated from UCLA's prestigious School of Theater, Film and Television with a BA in theater and a minor in film. Since graduating she has written, produced, and starred in her own comedic web series called Losing It (*www.losingitseries.com*). She is also part of the comedy duo Miss Understood, whose videos you can check out on YouTube. Additionally, Samantha is an improv performer who can occasionally be seen making a fool of herself onstage at various venues in Los Angeles. When she's not writing or performing comedy, Samantha likes to eat copious amounts of food and pet the fluffiest animals she can find. To view her hilarious, mostly food-centric tweets, check her out on Twitter *@samcardona*.

KEISHA COSAND was born in McAllen, TX. Her family moved quite a bit, starting in the Rio Grande Valley in Texas, then moving to Yakima Valley in Washington State, and finally, to the San Joaquin Valley in California. She spent her teen years in Fresno, and completed her BA and MA in English at California State University, Fresno, where she was mentored by writers Liza Wieland and Steve Yarbrough. As soon as her degree was finished, she decided she'd had enough of the valleys and headed south to the beach. Keisha is a professor of composition, literature, and creative writing at Golden West College, in Huntington Beach, CA. She is a short-story writer, poet, and dramatist. Her most recent work appears in *Words, Pauses, Noises* and *YAY! LA Magazine*. She lives in Huntington Beach with her husband, two young daughters, and gigantic yellow lab, Numan.

KIM CURRIER is a Chicago native currently living in Los Angeles. She is a big believer in books, television, and naps. You can find her on Twitter *@KimCurrier*.

JENNIFER DICKINSON received her BA from Hollins University. Her short fiction has appeared in *Blackbird*, *Other Voices*, *Word Riot*, and *Mason's Road*. She is the recipient of a Hedgebrook residency and a grant from the Money for Women/Barbara Deming Memorial Fund. She lives in Los Angeles where she wrote *Girls Like Us*, the play from which the monologues appearing in this book are excerpted, and is writing a novel about teenaged girls.

BRANDON ECON studied Magic: The Gathering and theater at the University of Utah in Salt Lake City. He has a cat named Katan, and you may have seen him shouting on stages all across Los Angeles. He is currently writing a trashy novel set in a sugar shack in Quebec, and a comedy horror film about a werewolf who writes other people's biographies. He voiced a Swedish paper bag puppet in a Fandango commercial and recently built a spice rack, which he is very proud of. He was born in Ohio but doesn't like to talk about that. A werewolf wrote this.

DAISY FAITH is a comedic actor and writer who lives in Los Angeles. She has advanced training from The Groundlings and the Upright Citizen's Brigade as well as The Nerdist School, where she's currently on a house team. As an actor she's appeared on *How I Met Your Mother*, *Pretty Little Liars*, *Conan*, *Days of Our Lives*, and *Nashville*. Find her on Twitter *@DaisyFaith* and at *www.DaisyFaith.com*.

MARGARET FINNEGAN is the author of *The Goddess Lounge* (a novel that is very funny) and *Selling Suffrage* (a history of the women's suffrage movement that is very serious). Her work has appeared in *Salon*, *Los Angeles Times*, *FamilyFun*, and other publications and anthologies. She teaches writing at California State University, Los Angeles, and she would like you to know that she once owned a complete set of original *Star Wars* action figures. In a fit of *Toy Story*–induced insanity, she gave them all away. She realizes that was a big mistake. Learn more about Margaret on her website *www.MargaretFinnegan. com*. You can also follow her on Twitter *@FinneganBegin* and on Facebook at *www.facebook.com/authorMargaretFinnegan*.

JESSICA GLASSBERG is a comedy writer and stand-up comedian. For ten years, she was the head writer on *The Jerry Lewis MDA Telethon* and performed stand-up on the nationally syndicated show five times. She has also written for Disney XD, "A Hollywood Christmas at The Grove" for Extra, and The Screen Actors Guild Awards (where her jokes were highlighted on E!'s *The Soup*, EntertainmentWeekly.com, and Hollywood.com). Additionally, Jessica was a featured performer on *The History of the Joke with Lewis Black* on the History Channel. Jessica's monologues have also been published in the books *Women's Comedic Monologues That Are Actually Funny*,

Men's Comedic Monologues That Are Actually Funny, and *Teen Boys' Comedic Monologues That Are Actually Funny*. She currently produces and hosts a stand-up comedy showcase in Los Angeles, "Laugh, Drink, Repeat." Jessica is also a prolific digital writer, with her work featured on HelloGiggles.com, Reductress.com, HotMomsClub.com, Kveller.com, AbsrdCOMEDY.com, attn.com, and Torquemag.io. For upcoming shows, clips, and writing samples, check out *www. jessicaglassberg.com* and follow her on Twitter *@JGlassberg*.

ANDY GOLDENBERG knows a lot about women. Look him up on the Internet: he's a real Ladies Man. He also knows that bios are super boring. He's five feet nine inches of Floridian Hunk and enjoys writing, sunsets on the beach, and stargazing. He's totally famous on YouTube. His Goldentusk Channel (*youtube.com/goldentusk*) has been viewed 51 million times. He was a cover boy on the Nice Jewish Guys Calendar, dressed as a woman for four months in Adam Sandler's *Jack and Jill*, and you'll just love his curly hair. If you run out of material from this book, he encourages you to challenge yourself and perform this bio. Follow him on Twitter *@goldentusk*.

RYANE NICOLE GRANADOS is a Los Angeles native and she earned her MFA in creative writing from Antioch University, Los Angeles. She received her BA in English from Loyola Marymount University, where she earned the Nikki Giovanni writing award and the honorable distinction of valedictorian for her graduating class. Her work has been featured in various publications including *PaniK*, *On the Brink*, *Dirty Chai*, *Gravel*, *Role Reboot*, *For Harriet*, and *The Manifest-Station* and is forthcoming in *Specter* magazine. Additionally, she teaches English at Golden West College and has authored a student success manual entitled *Tips from an Unlikely Valedictorian*. Ryane is best described as a wife, writer, and mom who laughs loud and hard, sometimes in the most inappropriate of circumstances. As a result, she hopes the completion of her first fiction novel will inspire, challenge, amuse, and motivate thinking that cultivates positive change. More of her work can be found at *ryane-granados.squarespace.com* or on Twitter: Ryane Granados *@awriterslyfe*.

DEREK HEEREN is a mild-mannered businessman by day and sleep enthusiast by night. Between all that sleeping and businessing, he is an actor, a writer, and an award-winning editor (awarded from a small film festival in 2002, but he still counts it!) From the age of nine, Derek began writing (but not finishing) a variety of short stories, novels, and homework assignments (a proud tradition that he continues to this day). Derek hails from Bloomington, MN, and went to college in St. Paul, where he graduated with a BA in theatre arts from Bethel College (which has, itself, now graduated to Bethel *University*). Currently, he lives in Los Angeles with his wife and two-year-old daughter, who both give him endless joy and writing material.

KATE HUFFMAN is an actor, writer, and comedian originally from Indianapolis, IN, and currently residing in Los Angeles. She actively works in film, television, and theatre in addition to writing, producing, and acting in online comedic shorts and web series. She is a proud member of the Elephant Theatre Company, where she has appeared in many productions, including *100 Saints You Should Know*, for which she won an LA Weekly Theatre Award and was nominated for an LADCC (Los Angeles Drama Critics' Circle) Award. In the comedy realm, Kate performs sketch and improv at the Upright Citizens Brigade Theatre, Improv Olympic West, and the Second City. She earned her BFA in Acting at the University of Miami, and generally speaking, thinks humans are pretty great.

JP KARLIAK is a voice-over artist, writer, solo performer, and snappy dresser who hails from the "Electric City," Scranton, PA.

His voice has fallen out of the mouths of Marvel heroes and villains, a werewolf nemesis of the Skylanders, and the self-proclaimed super genius Wile E. Coyote, among others. On screen, he planned a fancy party for Sarah Michelle Gellar and delivered singing telegrams to *The Real Husbands of Hollywood*. A graduate of the USC School of Theatre, iO West, and Second City Training Center, he has written numerous short films and plays produced in locales around the country. His full-length solo show, *Donna/Madonna*, has garnered awards at the United Solo, New York International Fringe, and San Francisco Fringe Festivals. He can always be found at fancy chocolate boutiques or on his website, *jpkarliak.com*.

LIZ KENNY is a wonky-eyed optimist, comedy writer, producer, and director, living in Los Angeles. She writes and performs comedy at The Nerdist, Upright Citizens Brigade, and the Clubhouse. Her sketches have been featured in the Northwestern University Alumni Showcase, and the iO Scripted Comedy Festival. Liz was a finalist in the 2013 Acclaim Television Writing Contest for her spec script of *Louie*, in which Louie tries to protect his daughter as she enters the sexual hurricane of adolescence. During the "business-like phase" of her career, Liz studied finance and international business at Georgetown; worked for a global bank in Chicago, Amsterdam, and New York; got her MBA at Kellogg; and became a strategy consultant for McKinsey & Co. She grew up in Chicago surrounded by a family that's still generating material for great stories! You can keep up with Liz on the tweets *@kizlenny*.

LINDA LANDEROS, originally from the Bay Area, used to be a teacher and taught overseas while in the Peace Corps. Clearly she set out to pursue a career in comedy! She currently lives in Los Angeles and writes sketch comedy for shows like *Top Story! Weekly*. She's also an actress and can be seen in film, TV, and around town in live sketch and improv shows.

ANGI LENHART is an actress, voice-over artist, producer, writer, and emoji poet. As a proud member of SAG-AFTRA and an alum of iO West, she has graced stage and screen, but it's her voice that has earned the most time on national TV, radio, and Internet campaigns. She has lived in Los Angeles since 2007, but her heart (and stomach) will always be in the Windy City. She will happily explain why Art of Pizza has the greatest deep dish and show you 182 pics of her pug, Jacob.

MOREEN LITTRELL is a writer, director, producer, author, and actress who has successfully made the transition from eighth-grade Class Clown to stand-up comedian. Originally from Coos Bay, OR, Moreen studied creative writing and film production at USC and Syracuse University, acting at the Beverly Hills Playhouse, improv at The Groundlings, and pattern making at the Fashion Institute of Technology. Besides being a contributing author to Alisha Gaddis's *Women's Comedic Monologues That Are Actually Funny* (July 2014) and *Teen Girls' Comedic Monologues That Are Actually Funny* (December 2015), Moreen is also the author of the roman à clef, *Lost in Manhattan*. After eight years in Manhattan, Moreen lives in Los Angeles for the third time, the charm. E-mail her night and day at *moreenlittrell@gmail.com*. She's got nothing better to do and could use the company.

BRI LeROSE is a Los Angeles–based writer and comedian. She was born in Racine, WI, where her notable accomplishments included a rousing speech to the school board and the role of "funny side character" in basically every play or musical ever. She is a graduate of Boston College and holds a master's degree in secondary English education from the University of Missouri, St. Louis. She wrote screenplays and sketch comedy in Boston before moving to St. Louis to teach a bunch of middle school kids about proper grammar. After that turned out to be only partially successful—she moved to Los Angeles to correct the grammar of adults. Since moving to Los Angeles, she's worked for MTV, The Toast, and Netflix, and told jokes to rooms of varying sizes and interest levels. You can find more of her writing at *www.brilerose.com* and more of her brain garbage on Twitter *@brilerose*.

LEAH MANN grew up in Washington, DC, and graduated with a degree in theater arts from Brown University in 2003. Since moving to Los Angeles in 2004, she has written several screenplays, television specs, short stories, and one novel that no one will ever see. Her short story "Going Solo" was published alongside work by prominent authors such as Neil Gaiman and Ray Bradbury in the horror anthology *Psychos: Serial Killers, Depraved Madmen and the Criminally Insane*. She is delighted to have a number of monologues included in *Men's Comedic Monologues That Are Actually Funny*. Leah currently works as a production designer, property master, and set decorator. She digs crosswords, her garden (get it . . . digs her garden . . .), and reads a lot of books. Since writing her bio for the men's monologue collection she has decided to get a dog. Find her online at *www.leahmann.com*.

SARAH McCHESNEY spent her childhood in the United Kingdom and moved to Pittsburgh, PA, during that time when children are the kindest and most understanding—middle school. While the horrors of that time are unspeakable, they helped her hone her skills as a comedian and writer at a very early age. Sarah now lives in Los Angeles working as a writer, producer, and performer. She is an alumna of both The Groundlings and The Upright Citizens Brigade where she can frequently be seen performing improv and sketch comedy. Sarah is also a member of the Jim Henson Company's *Puppet Up!—Uncensored*, a live stage show combining puppetry and improv. In addition to writing comedy, Sarah also writes science fiction and horror, and is passionate about creating roles for intelligent, funny, and adventurous women, no matter the genre. You can cyberstalk Sarah on Twitter *@wonkychez* and on her web at *www.sarahmcchesney.com*.

KATHARINE McKINNEY is a writer, performer, and social-media expert from Evansville, IN. Most recently she was the director of Evansville's inaugural *Listen To Your Mother Show* in May 2015. Kate gleans much comic inspiration from her four children and her husband, Hugh McKinney—the funniest man no one has ever heard of. Kate says she learned how to have a sense of humor when she stopped taking herself so seriously. Her piece was inspired by actual events (but we're not naming names!). The monologue in this book is Katharine's second piece for the Applause Acting Series; you can read her other piece in *Teen Boys' Comedic Monologues That Are Actually Funny*. Catch up with her at her blog *www.katharinemckinney.com* and follow her on Twitter *@katecake*.

MARISOL MEDINA is a writer, blogger, and comedian who takes pleasure in poking fun at American culture and the voices of its women. In a past life she was a dramatic actress before turning to comedy and graduating from The Groundlings in Los Angeles. She has since performed and written plays, short films, and live comedy acts and sketches at The Groundlings, Upright Citizens Brigade, Comedy Central Stage, SF Sketchfest, Los Angeles Comedy Festival, and The Comedy Store. Armed with a bachelors in drama from the University of Washington, Marisol hopes to one day have a pretentious discussion regarding nontraditional acting methods and the current state of live theater. For more of Marisol, visit her at *www.marisolmedina.com*.

KATE MICKERE is a writer and cake enthusiast based in Los Angeles. On the Internet, her writing can be found on XO Jane and within Hillary Carlip's *Find Me I'm Yours* story verse. Her play

Mod Party was recently produced by the Actor's Theatre of Louisville as a part of their Tens festival. Kate won the Alfred P. Sloan Student Screenwriting Award for *Capturing the Stars*, a screenplay about lady astronomy pioneers in the Victorian era. She holds an MFA in dramatic writing from Carnegie Mellon University. You can find more of her work (including her Elizabeth Taylor diet blog) at *www.katemickere.com* and *@katemickere*.

CHARITY L. MILLER is a multiple Emmy Award–nominated writer and producer of hilarious media (that no one ever watches). She's a perpetual student of the Upright Citizens Brigade and iO West Training Centers and graduate of the Second City Conservatory and Writing Programs. She also possesses three useless degrees from accredited universities with National Championship winning football teams. An interesting fact is that she has perfect standardized test scores . . . and is Black. (Stop being surprised, racists!) She is the sole writer and creator of the comedy phenomena *THIS IS NOT A TAN!* and *Period Panties*. Charity also writes for Second City, iO West, and UCB sketch shows. She survives as a freelance writer of satirical content, but occasionally you can experience her wit via "reputable" entities such as the Twitter. She volunteers her writing knowledge toward the tutelage of inmates in the California Department of Corrections and Rehabilitation. Her work published in this book is dedicated to her father.

JOANNA CASTLE MILLER is a playwright, essayist, and screenwriter and the founder and executive producer of Wait Don't Leave Productions (motto: Because Tragedy Sucks). She's also the blogger behind WTFLucy.com, a satirical feminist take on every episode of *I Love Lucy*. Joanna's work has appeared on NBC, PBS, the Food Network, VH1, and E! Entertainment, and her monologue web series debuted in the summer of 2015. Joanna writes and speaks regularly on productivity and the creative process.

Although born and raised in her beloved Memphis, she moved away to the Big Apple and graduated from New York University's Gallatin School of Individualized Study, with a concentration in dramatic writing and journalism. She enjoys spending time with her friends on the beach and taking long walks. She and her husband live in Los Angeles with their dog, Henry. Follow Joanna on Twitter *@jocastlemiller* and on the web at *joannacastlemiller.com*.

ORLY MINAZAD is a freelance writer and editor, humor essayist, and bad cook based in Los Angeles, CA. Her writing explores many subjects, from Los Angeles's arts and culture to examining her personal life growing up with Jewish Iranian immigrant parents and their love-hate relationship with America (and instant mashed potatoes). She's a contributor to *LA Weekly* and *Emmy* magazine and has shared her personal stories on The Nervous Breakdown, Blunt Moms, Zocalo Public Square, and in an anthology on the way. Next on her agenda is a stage play about a young Middle Eastern girl's pursuit to become an all-American weather girl. She has a master's degree in professional writing from USC for which she owes a lot of money to angry banks. She lives in hiding with her husband and son in Los Angeles. Follow her *@OrlyMinazad*.

CATHERINE NICORA is a lover of ice-cream cones and choco-late and kisses. (Real ones). A writer and a comedian. Living in Los Angeles. Find her online *@gettingbackwolf* and *comicrookie.tumblr.com*.

GINA NICEWONGER has been "writing in the moment" by performing improv comedy for over ten years. She has written and performed in shows at the Annoyance Theater and Improv Olympic in Chicago and, more recently, at various theaters throughout Los Angeles. In addition to her monologues that are in the men's and boy's editions of *Comedic Monologues That Are Actually Funny*, Gina has written one-acts produced by Studio C Artists and enjoys writing sketch comedy with the groups BBQ Committee, Chrissy and Gina, and Hot Lunch. When not making stuff up, Gina enjoys teaching elementary school.

RACHEL PAULSON is a writer from Tampa, FL. Meaning, she grew up on both the beaches and in the country, the best of both worlds. After finishing school in Florida, she made the move out to Los Angeles. Rachel is a published online writer, with her works appearing on sites the likes of SheWired, CherryGRRL, and iVillage. Most recently, she wrote the short films *Kleptos* and *The Chest*, the latter of which has just been accepted into the Cannes Short Film Corner competition. She is currently working on her first novel.

RACHEL POLLON What can we say about Rachel Pollon that you don't already know? She's worked in both the music and television industries, where highlights included making deep and lasting friendships, letting Sean Penn bum a whole pack of cigarettes even though she initially thought he only wanted one, and appearing in the background of a scene on television's *Frasier*, silently playing a coffee bar patron having a lively conversation. (She'll reenact this for you if you buy her a drink.) Her essay about trying to navigate a confusing romantic situation ("Change for a Ten") can be found in the book *The Beautiful Anthology*, and her work can also be read on TheNervousBreakdown.com, TheWeeklings.com, and her website, SeismicDrift.com. She truly appreciates your time and consideration. And feels uncomfortable referring to herself in the third person. Find her on Twitter *@RachPo*.

CARRIE POPPY is a writer, performer, and audio host from Los Angeles, CA. She completed her comedy studies at the prestigious Groundlings School of Improvisation, received her bachelor's degree in philosophy from University of the Pacific, and earned her master's degree in journalism from the University of Southern

California. Her comedy and journalism podcast, *Oh No, Ross and Carrie*, is regularly one of the top 100 podcasts in the United States. Carrie lives with her adopted dog, Ella, in Hollywood, eats a lot of curry, and owns a fully functioning stove. She started performing in high school and assures you that the only sure way to fail is to give up. You can reach Carrie on Twitter *@carriepoppyyes* or at her website, *www.carriepoppy.com*.

ALESSANDRA RIZZOTTI has written for *GOOD*, *Little Darling*, *Idealist*, *Takepart*, *Heeb*, *Smith*, *Hello Giggles*, *Reimagine*, and *The Neave*, and has been featured on The White House blog for her work on the editorial series *Women Working to Do Good*. Her pitch packets have helped writer Kirsten Smith (*Legally Blonde*, *10 Things I Hate About You*) sell two films to Paramount and ABC Family. She's also been published in three Harper Perennial books with her six-word memoirs, as well as in three monologue books for Hal Leonard/ Applause in collaboration with Grammy Award–winner Alisha Gaddis. At *Backstage Magazine*, Alessandra currently strategizes and writes Twitter chats (in which she's garnered seven million impressions) and edits casting notices, where she bridges the gap between filmmakers and actors. Find her online at *http://alessandrarizzotti.com*.

KATE RUPPERT used to be a teenager; she totally gets it. Now she's an adult and has just as many, but totally different, woes in life—like what to have for dinner, and what to wear to work so people think she looks cute but still take her seriously. She has a hairless cat named Smalls and a sick apartment in Queenz. And she still cares what her parents think.

KATE RYAN hails from Los Olivos, a small, boozy town just north of Santa Barbara, CA. She graduated from the University of San Francisco with a B.A. in English and a B.S. in BS. She writes twisted, apocalyptic fiction and self-deprecating nonfiction—sometimes for money! Visit her blog at *therevolutionelle.com*. You can also boost her self-esteem by following her on Twitter *@revolutionelle*.

CHRISSY SWINKO is a writer and performer in Los Angeles. She has written for and performed on several notable stages including the Comedy Central Stage, iO West, iO Chicago, The Second City Hollywood, Comedy Sportz Chicago, and more. She has studied writing and improv comedy with UCB, The Groundlings, The Second City, and the iO Theater. She grew up in Ohio and is a graduate of Denison University. Her hobbies include eating chocolate, reading, and watching movies. Find her online *@omg4reals* and at *www.ChrissySwinko.com*. She thanks you for reading and performing her monologue. Have fun out there and break a leg!

DANA WEDDLE is an actress/comedian/cat lover originally from Norman, OK. She now lives in Los Angeles, City of Dreams! She has trained at The Second City Chicago, UCB LA, iO West, and The Groundlings. Dana loves producing her original films and sketches and performs live improv and sketch comedy all around LA. Careful when turning on your TV—you may see her in a commercial or two! Dana is really into hugs, winning on game shows, and tirelessly campaigning for the addition of the breathtaking unicorn to the Apple emoji keyboard. Find her online *@MrCatLadyD* and at *www.danaweddle.com*.

ANDRA WHIPPLE is a writer, improviser, and comedy enthusiast who lives in Los Angeles with her imaginary pug, Winston. She has produced comedy festivals, written sketch shows, and even ridden a horse. She studies media representation of women and other underrepresented groups, and writes to celebrate all of the stories we haven't heard yet. She has presented her findings at symposiums full of serious people who nodded approvingly. She grew up in

Centerville, OH, where she once played a purple crayon in a play, and went to school at UC Irvine, where she led the fantastic Improv Revolution. You can read the latest about her and her projects on the worldwide web at *andrawhipple.com*, or tweet pictures of dogs at her *@whipsical*.

KATIE WILLERT is a writer and performer living in Los Angeles, CA. Her work can be seen on Cracked.com, Funny or Die, and UCBComedy.com. She performs at the iO West with her main stage sketch team DJ Faucet. Katie is also a financial planning enthusiast and creator of The Wealthy Ceative (*www.thewealthycreative.com*), a website aimed at helping creatives lead financially fulfilling lives. You can find her on Twitter *@kawillert*.

Acknowledgments

A lot of people are awesome. Some people are more awesome in regards to this book. They get extra thanks from Alisha Gaddis:

Thank you to Sara Camilli—best literary agent ever. WE ARE DOING IT!! xo

Thank you to all the contributing writers. You all put yourselves out there. It is hard to be funny, and extra super hard to be funny on paper in a particular format. You guys did it and it is amazing! Wow.

Thank you to Hal Leonard and Applause Acting Series. You guys have given me so much guidance, support, and freedom. I couldn't ask for more in a publisher. Thank you especially to the team—Marybeth Keating, Patty Hammond, and John Cerullo—you guys make everything better—everything! I really love working with you.

Thank you to my parents, Karen and Bob Gaddis. You often have no idea what I am doing (I do a lot of random things)—but you always support me, and that means everything.

Special thanks to my bro and sister-in-law, Grant and Sandy Gaddis (respectively). You guys are SO SUPPORTIVE and give the best over-the-phone reactions. We will always call you first.

Thank you to my family and friends. Obviously. You all are the best.

Thank you to my stepdaughter, Ella. Someday, you will be old enough to read ALL the monologues in this book—not just a select few. That day will probably come too soon.

And the super biggest thanks of all to my handsome husband, Lucky Diaz. Thank you for inspiring me in every way. You make me better each moment just by knowing you. I cannot thank you enough, but I will keep trying! Oh! And thank you for pouring me that glass of wine when I never thought I could finish this one! We did it and isn't she grand?! Love you!

Monologue and Scene Books

Best Contemporary Monologues for Kids Ages 7-15
edited by
Lawrence Harbison
9781495011771 .... $16.99

Best Contemporary Monologues for Men 18-35
edited by
Lawrence Harbison
9781480369610 .... $16.99

Best Contemporary Monologues for Women 18-35
edited by
Lawrence Harbison
9781480369627 .... $16.99

Best Monologues from The Best American Short Plays, Volume Three
edited by
William W. Demastes
9781480397408 .... $19.99

Best Monologues from The Best American Short Plays, Volume Two
edited by
William W. Demastes
9781480385481 .... $19.99

Best Monologues from The Best American Short Plays, Volume One
edited by
William W. Demastes
9781480331556 .... $19.99

The Best Scenes for Kids Ages 7-15
edited by
Lawrence Harbison
9781495011795 .... $16.99

Childsplay
A Collection of Scenes and Monologues for Children
edited by Kerry Muir
9780879101886 .... $16.99

Duo!: The Best Scenes for Mature Actors
edited by Stephen Fife
9781480360204 .... $19.99

Duo!: The Best Scenes for Two for the 21st Century
edited by Joyce E. Henry, Rebecca Dunn Jaroff, and Bob Shuman
9781557837028 .... $19.99

Duo!: Best Scenes for the 90's
edited by John Horvath, Lavonne Mueller, and Jack Temchin
9781557830302 .... $18.99

In Performance: Contemporary Monologues for Teens
by JV Mercanti
9781480396616 .... $16.99

In Performance: Contemporary Monologues for Men and Women Late Teens to Twenties
by JV Mercanti
9781480331570 .... $18.99

In Performance: Contemporary Monologues for Men and Women Late Twenties to Thirties
by JV Mercanti
9781480367470 .... $16.99

Men's Comedic Monologues That Are Actually Funny
edited by Alisha Gaddis
9781480396814 .... $14.99

One on One: The Best Men's Monologues for the 21st Century
edited by Joyce E. Henry, Rebecca Dunn Jaroff, and Bob Shuman
9781557837011 .... $18.99

One on One: The Best Women's Monologues for the 21st Century
edited by Joyce E. Henry, Rebecca Dunn Jaroff, and Bob Shuman
9781557837004 .... $18.99

One on One: The Best Men's Monologues for the Nineties
edited by Jack Temchin
9781557831514 .... $12.95

One on One: The Best Women's Monologues for the Nineties
edited by Jack Temchin
9781557831521 .... $11.95

One on One: Playing with a Purpose
Monologues for Kids Ages 7-15
edited by Stephen Fife and Bob Shuman with contribuing editors Eloise Rollins-Fife and Marit Shuman
9781557838414 .... $16.99

One on One: The Best Monologues for Mature Actors
edited by Stephen Fife
9781480360198 .... $19.99

Scenes and Monologues of Spiritual Experience from the Best Contemporary Plays
edited by Roger Ellis
9731480331563 .... $19.99

Scenes and Monologues from Steinberg/ATCA New Play Award Finalists, 2008-2012
edited by Bruce Burgun
9781476868783 .... $19.99

Soliloquy!
The Shakespeare Monologues
edited by Michael Earley and Philippa Keil
9780936839783
Men's Edition $12.99
9780936839790
Women's Edition $14.95

Teen Boys' Comedic Monologues That Are Actually Funny
edited by Alisha Gaddis
9781480396791 .... $14.99

Teens Girls' Comedic Monologues That Are Actually Funny
edited by Alisha Gaddis
9781480396807 .... $14.99

Women's Comedic Monologues That Are Actually Funny
edited by Alisha Gaddis
9781480360426 ...... $14.99

Prices, contents, and availability subject to change without notice.